D1293435

WHAT MUST I DO TO BE SAVED?

The Bible's Definition
of
Saving Faith

By Dr. Steven Waterhouse
Th. M., D. Min.

Westcliff Press
P.O. Box 1521, Amarillo TX 79105

Other Books By Steven Waterhouse

*Strength For His People, A Ministry For the
Families of the Mentally Ill*

The Sanctity of Life

*Not By Bread Alone, An Outlined
Guide to Bible Doctrine*

*Blessed Assurance, A Defense of the
Doctrine of Eternal Security*

First Edition 2000

Copyright 2000 by Steven W Waterhouse

Westcliff Press
P.O. Box 1521
Amarillo TX 79105
1-806-359-6362
westcliff@amaonline.com

ISBN: 0-9702418-0-1
Library of Congress Catalog Card Number 00-134708

Printed in the United States of America

Scripture taken from the New American Standard Bible,
Copyright The Lockman Foundation 1960, 1962, 1963, 1968,
1971, 1972, 1973, 1975, 1977, 1995
"Used by permission." [www.Lockman.org.]

About The Author

Dr. Steven Waterhouse has served as the Pastor of Westcliff Bible Church in Amarillo, Texas, since 1985. Dr Waterhouse has degrees from Dallas Theological Seminary (D. Min.); Capital Bible Seminary, Lanham MD (Th. M. in Hebrew and Greek); Spring Arbor College in Michigan (B.S. Social Science) and Cornerstone University in Grand Rapids.

This study is an excerpt from a detailed study on systematic theology written by Dr. Waterhouse entitled, *"Not By Bread Alone; An Outlined Guide to Bible Doctrine"*. Dr Waterhouse has also written *Strength For His People*: *A Ministry to Families of the Mentally Ill*, which offers a Biblical perspective on mental illnesses and other types of family problems. Thousands of copies of *Strength For His People* have been distributed, and requests continue to be received daily for the book. Pastor Waterhouse continues to exercise this ministry from Westcliff Bible Church, evangelizing and nurturing the relatives of those with severe mental illnesses. In addition, Dr Waterhouse is the author of *The Sanctity of Life*, research on God's View of the unborn, and *Blessed Assurance; A Defense of the Doctrine of Eternal Security*

Information about this book and others authored by Dr. Waterhouse can be accessed at his web site; www.webtheology.com

Acknowledgments

Many faithful servants of God labored on this
project. My own strength
would have failed without you.

Hugh Akin
Dan Bentley
Mary Daily
Dwight Davis
Alan Good
Janet Kampschroeder
Gabriel Trevizo

The congregation of Westcliff Bible Church,
Amarillo deserves praise for allowing
pastoral energies to be devoted to
Bible study and for the
financial backing of Bible research

Dedication

*For my co-worker, Marilyn, and
my own pastor, Merritt Johnson.
Pastor Johnson taught me the grace of God.
Marilyn has shown me the grace of God.*

Steven Waterhouse

Preface

Perhaps human pride explains the tendency to add something to the truth of salvation by faith alone. We gravitate toward the idea we can and must do something beyond admitting our helplessness and obtaining all from Christ. In efforts to increase visible results or misguided attempts to improve morality, the simple and clear gospel of faith becomes hazy.

Evangelists often demand public confession or else they claim a person cannot possess genuine faith. Saving repentance is misdefined to involve virtually a call to sinlessness. It is said, "If He's not Lord of all, He is not Lord at all." Evangelists use the appeal, "ask Jesus into your heart" though the Bible does no contain such language. Other variations nip away at the simple truth of faith in Christ alone. This booklet has not been written with a harsh attitude but with concern that believers realize the dangers of an unclear gospel. Fear of God and humility before Him demand adherence to His Word on this crucial doctrine.

WHAT MUST I DO TO BE SAVED

Table of Contents

Table of Contents

Continued:

If one browses a typical tract rack in a Bible-believing church, he may be surprised at the number of terms and phrases that are given as conditions for salvation. Gospel appeals come across variously as "believe," "repent," "confess," "deny self," "yield," "surrender," "receive," "accept," "make Jesus Lord," "ask Jesus into the heart," "forsake all," etc. Sometimes the terms are combined to give three, four, or five steps to salvation (e.g., first repent, then believe, then confess, and so forth). Do all of these terms mean the same thing? Is there one, or is there more than one, condition for salvation? Before a Christian is ready to witness, and certainly before an evangelist is equipped to speak in public, the question, "What must I do to be saved?" must be answered with precision!

Believe, Trust, and Exercise Faith

Many Scriptural texts present the only condition for salvation as being belief (synonyms: trust and faith). In fact, there are more than 150 New Testament passages where salvation is conditioned upon believing alone. If any other requirement is added, it will cause these verses to be incomplete and misleading. Therefore, all terms that express a condition genuinely necessary for salvation (such as repentance) must be interpreted as to be compatible with a salvation based upon faith alone. Terms that cannot be made compatible with faith alone as a condition for salvation are used improperly and dangerously at best and, at worst, are sheer heresy.

All Protestant theologians began with that basic
tenet of the Reformation, *sola fide,* faith alone. Here
are some of the key texts where the Bible declares
faith alone brings salvation:

- "For God so loved the world, that He gave
  His only begotten Son, that **whoever believes in Him** should not perish, but have
  eternal life" [John 3:16].

- "**He who believes** in Him is not judged; he
  who does not believe has been judged already, **because he has not believed** in the
  name of the only begotten Son of God" [John
  3:18].

- "Truly, truly, I say to you, he who hears My
  word, and **believes Him who sent me**, has
  eternal life, and does not come into judgment, but has passed out of death into life"
  [John 5:24].

- "For this is the will of My Father, that everyone who beholds the Son **and believes in
  Him**, may have eternal life; and I Myself will
  raise him up on the last day" [John 6:40].

- "Truly, truly, I say to you, **he who believes**
  has eternal life" [John 6:47].

- Jesus said to her, "I am the resurrection and
  the life; **he who believes in Me shall live**
  even if he dies, and **everyone who lives and
  believes in Me shall never die**. Do you believe this?" [John 11:25-26].

- Many other signs therefore Jesus also per-
  formed in the presence of the disciples,

which are not written in this book; but these have been written that you may believe that Jesus is the Christ, the Son of God; **and that believing you may have life in His name** [John 20:30-31].

- "[A]nd through Him everyone **who believes** is freed from all things..." [Acts 13:39].

- "Sirs, what must I do to be saved?" And they said, "**Believe in the Lord Jesus**, and you shall be saved, you and your household" [Acts 16:30-31].

- For I am not ashamed of the gospel, for it is the power of God **for salvation to everyone who believes**... [Rom. 1:16].

- ...even the righteousness of God through **faith in Jesus Christ** for **all those who believe**...[Rom. 3:22].

- ...whom God displayed publicly as a propitiation in His blood **through faith** [Rom. 3:25].

- For we maintain that a man is **justified by faith** apart from works of the Law [Rom. 3:28].

- ...since indeed God who will justify the circumcised by **faith** and the uncircumcised **through faith** is one [Rom. 3:30].

- But to the one who does not work, but **believes** in Him who justifies the ungodly, **his faith** is reckoned as righteousness...[Rom. 4:5].

- Therefore, having been **justified by faith**, we have peace with God through our Lord Jesus Christ [Rom. 5:1].

- For the Scripture says, **"Whoever believes** in Him will not be disappointed"....So **faith** comes from hearing, and hearing by the word of Christ [Rom. 10:11, 17].

- "[N]evertheless knowing that a man is not justified by the works of the Law but **through faith in Christ Jesus**, even we have **believed in Christ Jesus**, that we may be **justified by faith** in Christ, and not by the works of the Law; since by the works of the Law shall no flesh be justified" [Gal. 2:16].

- Even so Abraham **believed God**, and it was reckoned to him as righteousness. Therefore, be sure that it is those who are of faith who are sons of Abraham [Gal. 3:6-7].

- Now that no one is justified by the Law before God is evident; for, "the righteous man **shall live by faith"** [Gal. 3:11].

- But the Scripture has shut up all men under sin, that the promise **by faith** in Jesus Christ might be given to **those who believe** [Gal. 3:22].

- Therefore the Law has become our tutor to lead us to Christ, that we may be **justified by faith** [Gal. 3:24].

- For you are **all sons of God through faith** in Christ Jesus [Gal. 3:26].

- For by grace you have been **saved through faith;** and that not of yourselves, it is the gift of God; not as a result of works, that no one should boast [Eph. 2:8-9].

It is possible to accept the Scriptural fact that faith alone saves but give a wrong definition to faith. It is imperative that saving faith be accurately defined by Scriptural contexts.

The Hebrew Background
for the Meaning of Faith

With the exception of Dr. Luke, all the New Testament authors were Jews, and all the authors were conversant with the Old Testament. Their understanding of faith would be based upon the meaning of faith in the Old Testament.

The Hebrew word for "to believe" is *aman,* which relates to our word *Amen.* In some verbal stems (*qal/hiphal*), the word means "to be firm, to support, to be secure, to be faithful." B.B. Warfield, that great theologian from Princeton, says *aman* describes "whatever holds, is steady, or can be depended upon."[1] This definition is based upon observation of how *aman* is used in the Old Testament.

Aman (in the *qal* stem) is used of people who are caretakers for children who support and sustain them (support by literally carrying them or by financial support). The word means "foster father" or "nurse"

---

[1] Benjamin B. Warfield, *Biblical and Theological Studies,* ed. Samuel G. Craig, reprint ed. (Philadelphia: The Presbyterian and Reformed Publishing Co., 1968) 429.

in Num. 11:12; Ruth 4:16; 2 Sam. 4:4; 2 Kings 10:1, 5; Esth. 2:7; Isa. 49:23; Lam. 4:5. A guardian, nurse, nanny, or foster father, is someone on whom the infant utterly depends. He or she is reliable, trustworthy, dependable, firm, and supportive. *Aman is* used (in the *qal* stem) of door posts and pillars which are supportive, secure, firm, in 2 Kings 18:16 and with a negative in Jer. 15:18 to describe an unreliable stream.

Another grammatical form of *aman* (the *niphal)* yields the same meaning. The word refers to something that is firm, supportive, and dependable. Isaiah uses the word of a wall that can securely hold a nail in Isa. 22:23, 25 and of supporting children in Isa. 60:4. There are references to a stream that can be relied upon to provide water and not go dry in Isa. 33:16 and a kingdom that will be stable in 2 Sam. 7:16. When this form of *aman* is used of personal beings the meaning is that God can be depended upon to keep a promise (e.g., Deut. 7:9; Psa. 89:28) and that a treasurer can be relied upon in handling money (Neh. 13:13). These examples prove that the Hebrew word *aman* refers to firmness, dependability, faithfulness, trustworthiness, and reliability.

From these usages one would expect that the causative form of *aman* (the *hiphal*) means not so much to be firm, dependable so forth but to "**consider someone** or **something to be** firm, dependable, faithful, trustworthy, reliable." The change is from being a faithful one to **considering another** to be a faithful one. When we consider another to have these characteristics we are trusting them, depending upon them, relying upon them. This is a basic meaning to Hebrew ideas of faith. The specific meanings might range from intellectually accepting a fact to trusting upon a person.

Hab. 1:5 uses believe in the sense of to intellectually believe the truth of a message. Verses that seem to contain the idea of trust often use the phrase to **believe in**. The idea of trust seems to be included in these Old Testament references using *aman* (*hiphil* stem) Gen. 15:6; Ex. 14:31; Num. 14:11; Deut. 1:32; 9:23; 28:66; 2 Kings 17:14; 2 Chron. 20:20; Job 24:22; Psa. 27:13; 78:22; 106:24; Isa. 28:16; 43:10. Sometimes both the ideas of intellectually believing a fact and trusting a person are combined. In Num. 14:11, Deut. 1:32, and 9:23, belief is the opposite of the Israelite failure to invade Canaan from Kadesh-Barnea. In other words, they should have not only intellectually believed the message that God would give them the land, but also they should have trusted Him enough to begin the conquest. In Ex. 4:31 the people believed intellectually Moses' message that God was going to lead them out of Egypt, but they also believed in the sense of trust. In Isa. 7:9 Isaiah wants King Ahaz to believe intellectually in the prediction of deliverance from enemies, but he also wants the king to have confidence and assurance in God's gracious promise.

Contrasts and parallels help define a word. In Psa. 27:13-14 *aman* is parallel to hope and in Psa. 78:22 it is parallel to another Hebrew word that means trust. 2 Kings 17:14 and Deut. 9:23 show that faith is the opposite of rebellion, i.e., allegiance.[2] In Hab. 2:4, "the just shall live by faith," is contrasted with the pride exhibited by the insolent and self-assertive Babylonians. Thus, faith is humble dependence.

New Testament authors carry over these concepts of the meaning of faith into their teachings. Therefore, we would anticipate that to them faith in God would mean to consider God to be secure, firm, dependable and trustworthy. **Viewed from man's perspective this is called trust, confidence, dependence, and reliance.**

Saving Faith: What It Is Not

The New Testament is clear that saving faith is more than intellectual faith in certain facts about Jesus or orthodox doctrines (James 2:19; John 2:23-24; 3:2). Nicodemus believed in the existence of God and that Jesus was sent by Him as a miracle worker, but the Lord told him that he still needed salvation (John 3:3ff.). James reminds us that even demons intellectually believe in correct doctrine (James 2:19; see also Matt. 4:3; 8:29; Mark 1:34; 3:11; 5:7; Luke 8:28; Acts 16:17; 19:15).[3] Saving faith does indeed include a belief in certain key facts about Christ. Yet, saving faith is more than intellectual faith.

- You believe that God is one. You do well; the demons also believe, and shudder [James

---

[2] This study argues that saving faith can exist in a heart that is less than totally yielded to Christ's authority. However, this does not mean saving faith can exist with total rebellion.

[3] In Matt. 4:3 *if* means "since." Satan concedes that Jesus is the Son of God.

2:19].

If intellectual assent to doctrine is not saving faith, neither is the attitude that could be called emotional or temporal faith. Emotional faith is the kind of faith that the crowds expressed when they proclaimed Christ as their king on Palm Sunday (Matt. 21:1-11; Mark 11:1-11; Luke 19:28-40; John 12:12-19). In these accounts one reads of great emotional assertions about Christ. The crowd cried, "Blessed is the king of Israel!" "Blessed is He that comes in the name of the Lord" and "Hosanna to the Son of David." Nevertheless, one week later the same crowd shouted, "Let Him be crucified," "His blood be upon us and our children" (Matt. 27:22 and 25), and "We have no king but Caesar" (John 19:15). Why was there such a change?

The Jewish people on Palm Sunday were expressing an emotional or temporal faith. They wished to accept Jesus solely as a political deliverer from their present distresses, mainly the Romans. Earlier in His ministry the people were desirous of making Jesus king by force (John 6:15). They wanted Jesus to save them from their material needs, but that is all they really wanted from Him (John 6:26). They did not care about a spiritual Savior from sin. Christ resisted such an emotional and temporal faith. The crowds got all excited and were willing to believe He could deliver from temporal political problems, but there was no real spiritual interest in being saved from sin. This type of emotional faith is described as "seed on rocky places" in the parable of the sower. The message is received with emotional joy, but,

since there is no depth, the results are temporary
(Matt. 13:20-21; Mark 4:16-17; Luke 8:13). They
wanted a political savior, or a medical savior, or an
economic savior, but not a Savior from sin.

Today a person may desire Jesus to save them
from sickness, a broken relationship, combat, financial burdens, etc., and may genuinely believe He can
help in such temporal problems. They may even be
excited about it. Of course, it is neither wrong nor
unwise to want help from Christ for these trials, but
this type of faith by itself is not saving faith. If all a
person wants from Jesus Christ is that He will take
away a given temporal trouble, yet he could care less
about being saved from his sins, this is not saving
faith. Believing that Jesus can help in taking away a
problem is not the same as believing in Jesus as
Savior from one's sin and guilt. Many people respond
to high-pressure gospel invitations out of emotional
turmoil or confusion. They walk aisles with hearts
full of problems. They may even believe Christ can
solve these problems and may beg Him to do so. Yet,
if there is not also **trust** in Jesus Christ **to save from
sin**; then all that results is an emotional religious experience that makes one temporarily feel better about
life's problems. Such an emotional or temporal faith
in Jesus to make life better is not saving faith and
does not endure.

- "And those on the rocky soil are those who,
  when they hear, receive the word with joy;
  and these have no firm root; they believe for
  a while, and in time of temptation fall away"
  [Luke 8:13].

Saving Faith: What It Is

There are approximately 480 references to the verb *believe* and the noun *faith* in the New Testament. (*Faith* and *belief* are the same word in Greek.) An examination of each of these is impossible in such a limited study. However, they may be categorized into groups and discussed in a logical fashion.

Saving faith is more than intellectual adherence to certain facts and is more than an emotional attraction to Jesus believing He can be of assistance in temporal trials. Yet having said this, it must be stressed that genuine saving faith involves activity on the part of all three main components of the human soul: intellect, emotions, and will.

With the mind, a person must intellectually believe certain basic truths about the person and work of Christ. This is the **content** of saving faith. However, though a person believes the gospel is factually true with his mind, it is with his emotions that a person develops a conviction about the facts. He views them not only as true but also as an important need in his or her life. With emotions he gives assent to the value of the gospel and believes in it in a personal (as opposed to a strictly theological) way. The facts are not only deemed true but also personally needful and **relevant.**

The faith expressed by the mind and emotions is incomplete without the faith expressed by the will. With the will a sinner chooses to place confidence (trust, faith, reliance, dependence) in Christ and His shed blood, believing in Jesus Christ and the cross for salvation. It is the nature of saving faith that it also involves a choice to commit the soul's eternal destiny to Jesus Christ and His perfect work upon the cross. The mind, the emotions, and the will all play a role in genuine saving faith (though the process often takes place simultaneously). The definition of saving faith can best be studied under the three words indicated above (content, confidence, and commitment).

Saving Faith: Its Content

This section might be called the "**believe thats**" of the gospel. A person who believes that Jesus Christ was a guru or that He was merely a great religious teacher does not have saving faith because he is not believing in the "Biblical Christ." There have been, there are, and there will be many people who claim to be Christ. There are also many more that have great misconceptions about Jesus of Nazareth. While saving faith is more than an intellectual faith, the Scriptures are clear that saving faith does have its intellectual aspects. There is a content to saving faith. While a sinner does not need to know a complex doctrinal system, he must accept certain basic truths about Jesus Christ and the cross so that he believes in the Christ of the Bible and not a Christ of his own imagination or man's fabrication. The intellectual content of saving faith can be traced by following the phrase "believe that." Twenty times the Greek word for *believe* (*pistuo*) is followed by *that (hoti)*. This construction reveals the facts that must be believed intellectually in order to trust Christ.

A sinner must believe "that Christ died for our sins according to the Scriptures, that He was buried, and that He was raised on the third day according to the Scriptures" (1 Cor. 15:3-4; cf. Rom. 10:9-10; 1 Thess. 4:14). A sinner must believe "that Jesus is the Christ, the Son of God" (John 20:30-31; cf. John 8:24; 11:27). This involves accepting Him as Lord **in the sense of acknowledging His deity** (Rom. 10:9). A sinner must believe that Jesus Christ was sent from God (John 11:42; 16:27; 17:8, 21; 1 John 2:22) and that Jesus Christ is the Son of God who took upon Himself human flesh (1 John 4:2-3). Of course, the belief that one is a sinner and in need of help is implied in coming to Christ to find salvation.

These doctrines are the intellectual content of saving faith. To have saving faith one must believe in the Christ of the Bible. To have saving faith one must believe intellectually that Jesus Christ is the Son of God (deity), Lord, and Messiah who was sent from God. He must believe that God the Son took upon Himself flesh, died for our sins, and is now the risen Savior. If one claims to believe in God or be a Christian and yet denies the deity of Christ or the resurrection, he is either lying or is badly deceived.

Notice that saving faith does acknowledge that Jesus is God, and therefore, is also Master. **This is not the same as making a commitment to live for Him,** but there is the acknowledgement that Jesus, being the Master, does have a right to command.

Saving Faith: Its Confidence and Commitment

Saving faith has its intellectual content. However, when witnessing to others, a Christian is not just asking an unbeliever to believe Jesus was telling the truth or to cognitively accept certain facts about Jesus. The unbeliever is being urged to believe in, on, or upon Jesus Christ, meaning that he should place his **confidence**, trust, and reliance in Jesus Christ and His cross. Saving faith has its content, but it also places **confidence** in a person and His work: Jesus Christ.

In earthly matters one may place confidence in another person without committing his soul to that person. However, it is the nature of saving faith that its confidence in Christ must be expressed by and is inseparable from a **commitment of the soul's eternal destiny to Christ**. Although a person may recite and believe every fact in the apostle's creed, there is no salvation without a personal confidence in Christ and entrusting of the soul's safekeeping to Him.

How does one know that intellectual or emotional faith alone is not saving faith? How does one know that the type of faith that saves refers to confidence and commitment? The following points establish that the Greek word for belief has the range of meaning to specifically mean confidence, trust, and reliance, and they also show that this specific meaning is what the New Testament authors intended by saving faith.

The New Testament Word for *Faith* or *Belief* (*pistuo*, verb; *pistis*, noun) Can Specifically Mean

Confidence, Trust.

Previous material on the Hebrew word for *faith (aman)* proved that it could refer to trust, confidence, and reliance. When the New Testament verb for *to believe* is used in the Septuagint, it is always (except Prov. 26:25) a translation for *aman*. One can, therefore, safely assume that the New Testament authors felt that one of the specific nuances for the *pistuo* family is trust.

One hint from the New Testament itself that saving faith involves a commitment of the soul's destiny is that the Greek word *to believe* (*pistuo*) is translated "commit" (KJV) in John 2:24; Luke 16:11 (active forms) and Rom. 3:2; 1 Cor. 9:17; Gal. 2:7; 1 Tim. 1:11; and Titus 1:3 (passive forms). It means the same in 1 Thess. 2:4 where it is translated "put in trust." *To believe* in such contexts is to **entrust**.

Thus, both the Old Testament background and New Testament usage of *pistuo* (*to believe*) establish that one of the primary meanings of the term is to trust, to entrust, i.e., to have confidence, to commit something to someone because they are trusted. The following sections continue to establish that the specific meaning of **confidence** is not only a possible meaning for the term *believe*, it is the specific meaning the authors intended in connection with salvation.

The Command is not to Believe Jesus Christ but to Believe **in** Jesus Christ. This Refers to Confidence, Trust.

The Greek verb *to believe (pistuo)* often appears with prepositions. B. B. Warfield says of these prepositions, "When we advance to the constructions with prepositions, we enter a region in which the deeper sense of the word, that of **firm trustful reliance**, comes to its full rights."[4]

The truth of Warfield's conclusion may be realized by pondering that the gospel invitation is not just to believe Jesus Christ is telling the truth but rather to **believe in, on, or upon Jesus Christ** to be saved. The statement, "I believe the politician," means, "I believe he is telling the truth," i.e., not lying. However, the statement, "I believe **in** the politician," means not only that he is telling the truth, but also, "I have a personal confidence in his leadership and ideas." There is a great difference between believing Jesus and believing **in** Jesus. The later phrase expresses confidence and trust. It is striking that *believe in (pistuo* with *eis)* **is virtually unknown in secular Greek** but *believe* is followed by *eis,* the Greek preposition, indicating the goal or object of faith, **forty-nine** times in the New Testament. The New Testament authors must intend the contrast. They are purposely calling for a belief **in** Jesus Christ, not just a belief in facts about Him.

Among the forty-nine times where **believe** is followed by **in** *(i.e., pistuo* with *eis)* are these: John 1:12; 3:16, 18, 36; 6:29, 40; 11:25-26; 14:1, 12; 16:9; 17:20; Rom. 10:14; Gal. 2:16; 1 Pet. 1:8; 1 John 5:13. Twelve times *believe* is followed by *upon (pistuo*

---

[4] Benjamin B. Warfield, *Biblical and Theological Studies,* ed. Samuel G. Craig, reprint ed. (Philadelphia: The Presbyterian and Reformed Publishing Co., 1968) 437.

with *epi* followed by dative case five times and an accusative case seven times) as in Rom. 4:5, 24; Acts 9:42; 11:1; 16:31; 22:19. *Belief* is followed by another Greek word for *in (pistuo* with *en)* between one and three times depending on the manuscripts that are counted. The use of *pistuo* with these various prepositions reveals that the New Testament authors are urging **trust, confidence**, i.e., **and belief in** Jesus Christ in order to be saved. Usage with the above prepositions totals between sixty-three and sixty-five references. There are twenty times where *belief* is followed by *that*, *(pistuo* with *hoti),* and forty-five times where *belief* is followed by a dative. *(Pistuo* is used absolutely ninety-three times).

<u>Saving Faith Must Mean Confidence (Trust) by a Process of Elimination.</u>

One obvious way to establish that saving faith is confidence (which is expressed by a commitment of the soul's destiny to Jesus) is by elimination. It has already been shown that the New Testament clearly teaches that neither intellectual nor emotional faith is sufficient to save. Since the nuances of intellectual and emotional faith have been ruled out, the New Testament writers are stressing something more when they write of saving faith. They must have the specific meaning of **trust or confidence** in mind when they use the *pistuo* family in connection with obtaining salvation.

<u>Parallel Phrases Show that Saving Faith is the Equivalent of Confidence (Trust).</u>

Another method to show that the Bible means confidence (trust) when it refers to saving faith involves an examination of phrases that are parallel with and mean the same thing as believing in Jesus. Such expressions suggest confidence and commitment, not just an intellectual faith (which is merely the opposite of atheism). Believing in Christ for salvation is synonymous with having "committed (*one's soul* is implied) unto Him against that day" in 2 Tim. 1:12 (KJV), fleeing to Him as a refuge for protection in Heb. 6:18, coming unto God in Heb. 11:6, receiving or welcoming Jesus in John 1:12, looking unto Jesus for deliverance as the children of Israel looked to the bronze serpent in John 3:14, eating and drinking of Him both in John 4 and 6. These phrases speak of much more that intellectual adherence to a creed. They speak of a personal appropriation of the work of the cross, especially eating and drinking, and also of a personal relationship of confidence, entrusting oneself to Jesus Christ for deliverance and protection (flee to, look to, come to). Therefore, the meaning of saving faith must involve a **personal confidence in Christ** expressed by entrusting (committing) the destiny of ones soul to Him.

Believing in the Name Refers to Confidence (Trust) in Person of Christ.

A final reason that *belief* refers to confidence (trust) when used of saving faith lies in the appeal to "believe in His name" (John 1:12; 3:18; 1 John 3:23; 5:13). Are these verses teaching that salvation is granted to all who believe intellectually that there was a man named Jesus? That would be a nonsensical interpretation. In such contexts, *belief* must refer to having confidence, to trusting the person of Christ, rather than just believing the fact that there was a person named Jesus Christ.

Summary on Believe, Trust, Exercise Faith

Saving faith involves the mind, emotions, and will. With the mind the sinner must **believe that** Jesus Christ is the Son of God and Lord (i.e., God) who took upon Himself human flesh and was sent by God into the world as the Messiah to die for our sins and rise again. Saving faith entails these facts as its content. However, saving faith is more than believing intellectually certain basic facts about Christ. There is also an emotional assent in which a soul believes that these facts are not only true but also desirable, relevant, and personally needed.

Although intellectual belief in a content of facts about Jesus and emotional faith that these facts are personally needed are necessary to full saving faith, they are not sufficient. The gospel appeal is not just to believe facts about Jesus or to believe that He can help us, but to **believe in Christ**, i.e., to personally trust Him.

Saving faith exists when the will of a person commits the soul's eternal destiny to Christ and the cross, i.e., by an act of the will a person chooses to place his confidence in the Lord Jesus Christ and the finished work of the cross.

A deathly ill person may intellectually believe that a certain pill can save. He may emotionally believe that the pill is relevant to his own troubles. However, it is only when he chooses to depend upon the pill personally and expresses confidence in it by personal appropriation that a cure takes place. Salvation takes place when a person believes in the sense of personally appropriating the benefits of Christ's death by trust (i.e., confidence, reliance, dependence, and faith).

The sole condition for salvation is to trust in the Biblical Christ as Savior. All legitimate ways of communicating this one condition for salvation are either synonyms for faith or involve a specialized aspect of faith. All terms and phrases that are not compatible with faith alone as the condition for salvation are error.

Repentance as a Condition of Salvation
The Meaning of Repentance

The verb *repent* (m*etanoeo*) is used thirty-five times in the New Testament and the noun *(metanoya)* occurs twenty-two times. Usage is frequent in Luke, Acts, and Revelation. Probably most people think of "feeling sorry" or "feeling guilty" when they hear the term *repentance*. However, several considerations show that being sorry is not a synonym for repenting.

First, the word is a compound derived from *meta* meaning "to change" (as in metamorphosis) and *noeo* which refers to the mind (i.e., notion). Etymology indicates a basic meaning of "changing the mind." While sorrow often accompanies repentance and even promotes repentance, 2 Cor. 7:9-10 and Heb. 12:17 show that sorrow is not the same as repentance. Since 2 Cor. 7:9-10 teaches that sorrow can often lead to repentance, one must conclude sorrow is not exactly the same thing as repentance. Heb. 12:17 is even more clear. Esau is portrayed as being very sorry, to the point of tears, about selling his birthright. Nevertheless, he was unable to repent concerning the sale of his birthright for a bowl of lentil soup (Gen. 25:34). Repentance in Esau's case did not just mean feeling sorry (which he did), but rather it meant changing his mind about the sale (which he could not do). Repentance does not mean "feeling sorry" or "feeling guilty." It means "to change the mind."

Several times the Bible associates repentance with repudiation and departure from a former position. Acts 3:19 says, "repent therefore and return." Acts 26:20 contains the phrase "repent and turn to God" (see also Heb. 6:1 and Acts 8:22). Therefore, repentance involves turning away from something to something else. This must involve a change of mind because one may sorrow or feel guilty without ever repudiating a former idea or belief. When one repents of a belief and/or behavior, he must not only feel sorry but also change his mind about that issue. Therefore, repentance emphasizes a change of mind involving a turning away from something to something else.

To this point repentance has been defined. The next issue is whether or not the Bible teaches repentance is essential to salvation.

Repentance as a Necessity for Salvation

As long as it is properly defined to be compatible with *sola fide* (faith alone), repentance is a legitimate term to express the condition for salvation. This is evident from texts like the following: Luke 15:7, 10; Acts 2:38; 3:19; 17:30; 26:20 (verb repent); and Luke 15:7; 24:47; Acts 11:18; 20:21; 26:20; Rom.2:4; and 2 Pet.3:9 (noun, repentance).[5]

- "Therefore having overlooked the times of ignorance, God is now declaring to men that **all everywhere should repent**" [Acts 17:30].

- [A]nd He said to them, "Thus is it written, that the Christ should suffer and rise again from the dead the third day; and that **repentance** for forgiveness of sins should be proclaimed in His Name to all the nations, beginning from Jerusalem" [Luke 24:46-47].

- [T]he Lord is not slow about His promise, as some count slowness, but is patient toward you, not wishing for any to perish but for **all to come to repentance** [2 Peter 3:9].

The role of repentance in salvation gives rise to many questions. Since repentance involves a change of mind and turning away from a former position, what are the things from which an unsaved person must turn away in order to be saved? What are the truths about which a person must change his mind to be saved?

---

[5] Verses that contain John the Baptist's call to repentance are not included in this section. His call to repentance seems to have involved a preparation for the future salvation that the Christ would offer. More information on John the Baptist's call to repent and be baptized follows.

The object from which a person must repent is not the same in every passage. In Acts 2:38 and 3:19 Peter seems to be asking the Jews to change their minds about what they did to Christ by executing Him, i.e., to change their minds about who He is. Not everyone in the world was directly involved in the guilt of sending Christ to die in the same sense as these first century Jews. Therefore, this specific object of repentance, changing the mind about participation in Christ's crucifixion, would not be applicable to everyone. Heb. 6:1 mentions a changing of the mind about dead works. This object of repentance is applicable to all the unsaved in religions that teach that works are a means to salvation. However, the typical ex-atheist never believed in "dead works" in the first place because he never believed in the existence of a heaven for which man could work. Therefore, there is no need for the atheist to change his mind about dead works. People in different false religions and false philosophies with different backgrounds and ideas need to change their minds, i.e., repent, about different misconceptions. Acts 20:21 and 1 Thess. 1:9 mention that people must change their mind about God. Repentance about God is probably involved in every conversion. Yet, the specific ideas about which a sinner repents would be quite diverse. A Hindu definitely needs to change his mind about God to be saved. He must repent of polytheism. Yet, a change of mind about God would involve a different idea for a Satan worshipper or an atheist or an orthodox Jew. All must believe in Christ to be saved, but the misconceptions and hindrances that must be changed in order to believe are extremely diverse. In several places where repentance is linked with salvation, the object of repentance is **totally unspecified**: Acts 11:18; 17:30; 26:20; Luke 24:47; 2 Pet. 3:9.

Both logic and examples of Scripture indicate that, while some degree of repentance is involved in every conversion, the specific ideas or action about which a person must change his mind varies from person to person. An unsaved **person has to change the mind (repent) about anything that stands in the way of his coming to faith in Christ**. For some this will be a change about a philosophy, e.g., idol worship. For others this is a change of mind about sin, e.g., refusing to trust in Christ because they know He will command them to break off an immoral affair. The object of repentance is probably not the same in any two individuals. **A person must repent about whatever it is that keeps him or her from faith in Christ.**

Repentance and Evangelism

The fact that an evangelist does not know the precise falsehood of which a potential convert must repent should not be upsetting or confusing. Since the only condition for salvation is faith, it stands to reason that if faith is placed in Christ; then repentance has already occurred. When a person honestly and seriously entrusts his or her soul's eternal destiny to Christ, then that person has also changed his mind about whatever it was that had been a barrier to coming to Christ. Faith and repentance are not two separate conditions for salvation. Repentance is a particular aspect of saving faith. By trusting in Christ, the person has changed his mind, i.e., repented, about whatever kept him from accepting the Savior. The act of faith contains within it all the repenting that needs to be done to secure salvation. Faith in Christ includes both the specific objects that needed to be repented of and also the degree of repentance that needed to take place. By turning in faith to Jesus Christ, the soul has already fulfilled all the "change in thinking" and "turning away from" that is required for salvation. It is true that repentance is required of everyone for salvation, but the specific type of repentance varies with individuals and is ultimately unknown to the evangelist. The responsibility of the evangelist is to teach that the person must trust in Christ (and obviously this implies he or she must change their mind about anything that hinders faith in Christ). It is not the business of the evangelist to determine the specific ideas or sins that pose the barrier or for him to make a list of items from which a person must turn. If there is a "turning to" Christ, then the specific "turning away from" will take care of itself. (See Acts 3:19; 20:21; 26:20; 1 Thess. 1:9.)

"Repentance" vs. "Forsaking Sin" as a Prerequisite for Salvation

There must be caution or the term *repentance* will be misused to create a salvation based upon works. We dare not tell a potential convert that there must be a turning away from sins A, B, and C before there can be salvation. Salvation is based upon faith alone. If a person can believe, then he has already repented of whatever hindered faith and that is all the repentance he needs for salvation. No one has any authority to add more as a basis for salvation.

The Bible does not make the cessation of sin in general or of a specific sin, such as alcoholism, a prerequisite for salvation. This would not only be a works method for salvation, but it would be an impossible method for salvation. Asking a potential convert to overcome an addictive sin before conversion is asking him to obtain victory when he has absolutely no power to overcome sin. The command "to repent" is not the same as a command "to cease" all sin or any given sin before there can be salvation. Furthermore, the Bible never requires a person to promise to cease a particular sin in order to find salvation. Repentance should not be confused with a vow to stop or a promise to cease a particular sin that especially tempts an individual. Asking for a commitment to cease from a sin is asking for a commitment that cannot be made at a pre-conversion stage. There is no power in the life to make such an unrealistic promise. In fact, the appeal for a vow to stop sinning encourages the unsaved to have confidence in their own abilities, and that is the opposite of saving faith. A potential convert should be made to see that he has absolutely no ability to overcome sin and that he cannot in good faith even promise to forsake it. He is hopelessly dominated by sin. That is why he must believe in Christ. Salvation is based upon an empty hand that takes God's blessing as a free gift: "nothing in my hand I bring, simply to Thy cross I cling". Salvation is not based on a full hand that makes offers to God in order to have eternal life.

Repentance and Lordship Salvation

The concept of "Lordship Salvation" will be covered separately. It is enough to say here that there is nothing in the term *repentance* that involves what is commonly called Lordship Salvation. Telling a person that he must cease from sinning or promise to cease from sinning before he can have salvation is putting an impossible obstacle in front of him and adding to the one condition for salvation. An unsaved person who has tried repeatedly and unsuccessfully to break a sinful addiction does not have, nor does he understand, the power of Christ which comes after salvation. He might have enough faith to trust in Christ for salvation but lack the faith in self to promise to forsake a given dominating sin. There may be enough faith to trust in Christ, but the person feels that he cannot honestly make any promise to forsake sin because he has never been able to overcome it in his pre-conversion life. To people such as this, asking that they promise to forsake sin is useless and hypocritical. By misunderstanding repentance, some Christians make such hopeless people feel they cannot meet God's condition for salvation. Although they might believe in Christ, they know they are unable to promise a cessation from sin. The misunderstanding of repentance and the demand for a pre-conversion cessation from sin, or for a vow to cease sinning, creates an additional and heretical condition for salvation. In fact, it is best if an unbeliever feels utterly hopeless about overcoming slavery to sin. It is best if he realizes that he himself cannot forsake sin or promise to forsake sin and that he needs divine help. **All God requires from a sinner is that he wants deliverance from sin badly enough to trust in Christ for it.**

It is logical that every convert wants deliverance from sin in at least some unknown degree. It is also logical, since salvation involves believing Christ is God, that every convert acknowledges that Christ does have a right to direct the individual's life by virtue of being God. Therefore, it is true that saving faith cannot co-exist with a total rebellion against Christ's rule as Master or with an absolute lack of desire for deliverance from sin. However, this is not at all the same as concluding that there must be efforts to obey Christ as Master or commitments which promise a cessation from sin and a yielding to Christ's authority before salvation. The sinner indeed acknowledges Christ's authority by virtue of believing in the deity of Christ. However, he is not required to follow that authority or promise to follow it before he can be saved. God does not require so much of sinners to be saved. Neither should we. If a potential convert can **trust in** Christ, he has recognized Christ's authority to a sufficient degree; he has made all the commitments he needs to make, he has desired all the deliverance from sin he needs to desire, and he has done all the repenting that needs to be done in order to have salvation.

We dare not incorrectly define repentance so that it adds any requirement to *faith alone* for salvation. Repentance means "to change the mind." If a person can arrive at the point of trusting Christ, he has already repented (i.e., changed his mind about/turned away from) of whatever ideas or behavior that prevented faith in Christ. This is all God requires both as to the type of repentance and degree of repentance.

Summary on Repentance as a Condition for Salvation

When it is properly defined, repentance is a genuine condition for salvation. It is not only compatible with the term faith; it is a part of faith. In turning to Christ, there must be a turning away from all that hindered faith. Repentance is distinguishable but not separable from saving faith. The founder of Dallas Seminary wrote this about repentance:

> "It is true that repentance can very well be required as a condition of salvation, but then only because the change of mind which it is has been involved when turning from every other confidence to the one needful trust in Christ. Such turning about, of course, cannot be achieved without a change of mind. This vital newness of mind is a **part of believing**, after all, and therefore it may be and is used as a **synonym for believing at times**...."[6]

Conversion as a Condition for Salvation

---

[6] Lewis Sperry Chafer, *Chafer Systematic Theology*, vol. 7 (Dallas, Dallas Seminary Press, 1948) 7:265. Emphasis mine.

Though *be converted* is not used as frequently as other terms, it does express a legitimate condition for salvation as long as it is properly defined. The Greek word for *to convert* is used between thirty-six and thirty-nine times depending on the manuscripts that are counted. From its usage in non-salvation passages, one can tell it means "to turn toward" or "to turn back" (e.g., Matt.12:44; 24:18; Mark 5:30; 8:33; 13:16; Luke 8:55; 17:31; John 21:20; Acts 9:40; 15:36; 16:18; Gal. 4:9; 2 Peter 2:22; Rev. 1:12). When a person trusts in Jesus Christ for salvation, he is turning to Him for salvation. Thus, saving faith equals conversion in the sense of turning to Christ in faith for salvation and, also, turning back to God from whom all have strayed (Isa. 53:6).

Usually, the Bible does not use the command "be converted" in evangelistic appeals as a condition for salvation as it does in Acts 3:19. It is far more common that a Biblical author refers **back** to the time of salvation and calls it conversion or refers to a **third party's** conversion or lack of conversion (Matt. 13:15; Mark 4:12; John 12:40; Acts 9:35; 11:21; 15:19; 26:18, 20; 28:27; 2 Cor. 3:16; 1 Thess. 1:9 and 1 Pet. 2:25). In other words, it is more common for the Bible to use the word *conversion* to teach saved people what has happened when they believed than it is for the Bible to appeal to the unsaved to have a conversion. *Conversion* must be defined as "turning to Christ in saving faith" and must not be misunderstood to mean to add anything to faith alone as the one condition to salvation. *Conversion* simply means saving faith. It does not mean a person must totally change his lifestyle before salvation is granted. Conversion is turning to Christ in faith for salvation.

Receive or Accept Jesus as Savior

This term is not prominent as a Biblical condition for salvation, but it does occur in John 1:12.

> But as many as **received** Him, to them He gave the right to become children of God, even to those who **believe** in His name [John 1:12].

John 1:12 is quite clear that receiving Jesus Christ is the same as believing on His name. The meanings are the same. *Believe* gives more emphasis upon the active nature of saving faith. We must choose to trust Christ. *Receive* emphasizes more the passive aspect of saving faith. We must, by believing, be willing to receive a free salvation from Jesus Christ. *Believe* and *receive* are the same condition for salvation viewed with a slightly different emphasis. If by receiving or accepting Jesus Christ as Savior, we mean to trust in Him and His work on the cross, then it is proper to use the appeal to "receive or accept Christ as Savior."

Believe and Work to Earn Salvation

There are few errors that are more widespread and dangerous than the misconception that either works or religious rituals (or both) are conditions for salvation. On the positive side, this study has already demonstrated that over 150 Biblical texts condition salvation upon faith alone! If one adds works or rituals to faith, these passages would all be rendered contradictory and those who gave them would be liars (including the Lord Jesus Christ). Paul responded to the Galatian tendency toward a works salvation in some of the harshest language in the entire Bible. The position that salvation can be earned by works is an "arch-heresy." It can not be opposed too strongly!

But even though we, or an angel from heaven, should preach to you **a gospel contrary** to that which we have preached to you, let him **be accursed.** As we have said before, so I say again now, if any man is preaching to you **a gospel contrary** to that which you received, let him be **accursed** [Gal. 1:8-9].

- For all of us have become like one who is unclean, and all our righteous deeds are like a filthy garment [Isa. 64:6].

- They said therefore to Him, "What shall we do, that we may work the works of God?" Jesus answered and said to them, "This is the work of God, that you believe in Him whom He has sent"[John 6:28-29].

- [A]nd through Him everyone who believes is freed from all things, from which you could not be freed through the Law of Moses [Acts 13:39].

- [B]ecause by the works of the Law no flesh will be justified in His sight; for through the Law comes the knowledge of sin [Rom. 3:20].

- For we maintain that a man is justified by faith apart from works of the Law [Rom. 3:28].

- But to the one who does not work, but believes in Him who justifies the ungodly, his faith is reckoned as righteousness [Rom. 4:5].

- [B]ut Israel, pursuing a law of righteousness, did not arrive at that law. Why? Because they did not pursue it by faith, but as though it were by works. They stumbled over the stumbling stone [Rom. 9:31-32].

- But if it is by grace, it is no longer on the basis of works, otherwise grace is no longer grace [Rom. 11:6].

- [N]evertheless, knowing that a man is not justified by the works of the Law but through faith in Christ Jesus, even we have believed in Christ Jesus, that we may be justified by faith in Christ, and not by the works of the Law; since by the works of the Law shall no flesh be justified [Gal. 2:16].

- Now that no one is justified by the Law before God is evident; for, "the righteous man shall live by faith" [Gal. 3:11].

- For by grace you have been saved through faith; and that not of yourselves, it is the gift of God; not as a result of works, that no one should boast [Eph. 2:8-9].

- [W]ho has saved us, and called us with a holy calling, not according to our works, but according to His own purpose and grace which was granted us in Christ Jesus from all eternity [2 Tim. 1:9].

- He saved us, not on the basis of deeds which we have done in righteousness, but according

to His mercy, by the washing of regeneration
and renewing by the Holy Spirit [Titus 3:5].

- [H]ow much more will the blood of Christ,
  who through the eternal Spirit offered Himself without blemish to God, cleanse your
  conscience from dead works to serve the
  living God? [Heb. 9:14].

There are texts in the Scriptures that can be misinterpreted so as to establish that salvation is conditioned upon good works. However, the interpreter
still must face the facts that over 150 verses condition
salvation upon faith alone and that the New Testament is adamant about the truth that works do not
lead to salvation. The solution, in those texts that
seem to indicate that salvation comes by merit, is
simply to find another equally valid interpretation
that is compatible with faith alone as a condition for
salvation. In fact it will nearly always be the case that
the interpretation that makes the text compatible with
the rest of Scripture will also be the one that better
fits the context and the author's own ideas elsewhere.

As an example, consider James 2:26: "...faith
without works is dead." Of course, this passage can
be stubbornly interpreted as being contradictory to
the verses that are typed above in this section. Yet, it
can and should be interpreted to be consistent with
them. In the context, James had defined faith as intellectual faith in certain orthodox facts about God,
specifically monotheism: "You believe that God is
one. You do well, the demons also believe and shudder" [James 2:19]. Verse 26 simply means that an
intellectual faith in certain facts about God is not

enough for salvation. The type of faith that is genuine saving faith is the type that results in good works. A valid paraphrase would be "The type of faith that is just a belief in facts about God and never results in works is dead."

The resulting theology is not in contradiction to the "faith alone" doctrine emphasized by Paul and developed under the definition of saving faith in this book. James had previously asked in v. 14, "Can that [type of] faith save him?" James answers, "No," and Paul would have also agreed. Intellectual faith alone does not save. Paul would have also agreed that genuine saving faith results in good works (Eph. 2:8-10). When the term *faith* means intellectual acceptance of correct doctrine, as in James 2, then faith alone does not save. When the term *faith* means trust, reliance, confidence, as in Paul's writings, then such faith saves and also results in good works. The interpreter must notice that James and Paul use the term *faith* with different shades of meanings.

James 2 teaches that intellectual faith does not save. However, it does not and should not be used to disprove that faith alone (defined in the sense of trust) is insufficient to obtain salvation. When careful attention is given to the precise definition each author employs, these statements in James are not contradicting that faith (in the sense of confidence) saves. Every text that seems to be teaching a works salvation is better interpreted in ways that make it compatible with salvation by faith alone.

Believe and be Baptized to Obtain Salvation

If the reader is beginning to read at this point, it would be beneficial to go back and study previous research that establishes that God's only condition for salvation is faith. Also, it is pertinent to consider the preceding section that established that works and/or religious rituals do not save.

If some verses are studied in isolation from the rest of Scripture, they could be taken to prove that baptism is essential to salvation. However, it is just as true that these same texts can also be interpreted to be compatible with faith alone as a condition for salvation. Obviously, the correct interpretation is that which harmonizes all Scriptures rather than the one that causes contradictions between Scriptures. Since over 150 verses give faith alone as the condition for salvation, baptism cannot be viewed as a requirement for salvation (though baptism is a requirement for complete obedience to God.)

It is common to bring the examples of Jesus (John 4:2) and Paul (1 Cor. 1:17) into a discussion of baptism and salvation. Neither was personally involved in baptizing others to a great degree. Paul stated that his God-given task was to preach the gospel (the Greek word means "evangelize") rather than emphasizing baptism. Also, the thief on the cross is an example of one who obtained salvation without baptism (Luke 23:43), and Cornelius was clearly saved before

he was baptized (Acts 10:47).[7] These points are legitimate. However, they are secondary to the main
fact that baptismal regeneration would make the
Scriptures a massive contradiction. If salvation is by
faith alone, nothing can be added to it. If the trou-
bling texts can be interpreted in any way that is compatible with faith alone as a condition for salvation,
then that would be the correct interpretation. The rest
of this section will show that texts commonly used to
prove baptism is essential to salvation are really quite
compatible with the view that faith alone saves.

Mark 16:15-16

- And He said to them, "Go into all the world
  and preach the gospel to all creation. He who
  has believed and has been baptized shall be
  saved; but he who has disbelieved shall be
  condemned."

There is a real probability that this portion of
Mark was not in the original New Testament. Most
modern translations and commentaries will mention
the point that Mark 16:9ff. are not found in the oldest
existing manuscripts.

However, even if we assume these statements to
be genuine, they can be interpreted to be compatible
with faith alone. The last part of verse 16 shows that
disbelief (rather than lack of baptism) is the sole con-

---

[7] The thief on the cross technically died before Christian baptism
had been initiated. However, he did live during the period in
which John the Baptist's baptism was being commanded. Therefore, his example still gives a parallel that one can be saved without baptism.

dition that brings about eternal condemnation. Thus, it is belief that brings salvation. Verse 16a is true and correctly lists both belief and baptism as responses that God requires. It is teaching that God wants both belief and baptism, and that those who comply are saved. Yet, it is still possible to view that, of these two genuine requirements, belief is the sole element that brings about salvation. The interpreter's options are either to take Mark 16:16 in this manner or cause it to be a contradiction to many clearer passages of Scripture.

John 3:5

- Jesus answered, "Truly, truly, I say to you, unless one is born of water and the Spirit, he cannot enter into the kingdom of God."

Many views can be adopted of John 3:5 that would make it compatible with faith alone as a condition for salvation. For the purpose of this study, it is not important which is the best. As long as the verse can be legitimately taken in ways other than requiring baptismal regeneration, the result is the same, i.e., there is no proof that baptism regenerates.

Some take water to refer to physical birth (i.e., the water sack around an infant) because verse 6 contrasts physical birth with spiritual birth. Another grammatical possibility is to view the construction as a "hendiadys." This would make the translation read, "unless one is born of water, even the Spirit." Thus, water would be a symbol for the Holy Spirit. Precedent for associating the Holy Spirit with water is in Ezek. 36:25-27; Isa. 44:3; John 7:38-39; Titus 3:5. A third view would see water as a symbol for the Word of God. It is true that the Holy Spirit uses the Word to bring about the new birth (James 1:18; 1 Pet. 1:23) and that water is associated with God's Word in other Scriptures (John 15:3; Eph. 5:26).

Finally, it is even possible to take water as referring to John's baptism and still not read baptismal regeneration into the statement. John the Baptist's baptism is different than Christ's baptism. It is not even being practiced today.[8] However, it was at the time of John 3, and Nicodemus observed that John and Jesus were requiring people to be baptized. Perhaps John 3:5 is Christ's way of teaching that baptism alone is not sufficient. A paraphrase might be as follows: "Nicodemus it is true that I require my followers to be baptized. Yet, if that is all they have, they will not enter the kingdom of God. I require John's baptism, but the requirement to enter the kingdom of God is being born of the Spirit." If this interpretation is correct, then Christ is teaching that while John's baptism was God's will, it is the new birth by the Spirit that brings salvation. Nicodemus should not think that the ritual alone (though it was required) had any saving merit. Salvation is a work of the Spirit giving new life on the basis of faith (see John 3:16 in context). Thus, water could be under-

---

[8] John was baptizing people as a preparation to accept the Messiah's earthly ministry and kingship. As a nation, Israel rejected the Lord's earthly rule at His first coming. Thus, John's preparatory baptism has ceased. Christian baptism, based upon the Lord's death, burial, and resurrection, is different than John's baptism.

stood as being baptism in John 3:5 without making
the text teach baptismal regeneration. In fact Jesus
would be saying the opposite. Though He approves
of John's baptism, he wants clear understanding that
baptismal water does not save. Nicodemus was
taught that only life from the Spirit though faith
causes salvation.

The main truth must not be lost in details. John
3:5 can be interpreted in ways that do not teach that
baptism is a requirement for salvation. Regardless of
which view is preferred, all of them make John 3:5
compatible with clear texts that teach salvation is by
faith alone.

Acts 2:38

- And Peter said to them, "Repent, and let each
  of you be baptized in the name of Jesus
  Christ for the forgiveness of your sins; and
  you shall receive the gift of the Holy Spirit."

This verse is a favorite of those who think baptism
is a condition for salvation. However, it can also be
interpreted to fit nicely with the *sola fide* (faith alone)
position. The word *for* has many usages. One of its
meanings is "because of." In the sentence, "The police arrested him for shoplifting," it is evident that *for*
means "because of." The police arrested him because
of shoplifting. The Greek word *eis*, which is translated "for" in Acts 2:38, also has a wide range of
meanings. Like the English word *for*, e*is* can mean
"because of." Matt. 12:41 speaks of the men of Nine-
vah and says: "they repented (e*is*) the preaching of
Jonah." (The people repented **because** of the

preaching of Jonah.) The same meaning prevails in Luke 11:32. It is also possible that *eis* means "because" in Matt. 3:11, which reads: "I baptize you in water for (*eis*) repentance." A good understanding of John's statement would be, "I baptize you with water **because of** your repentance." (See also Rom. 4:20; 11:32; and Titus 3:14 for other possible causal uses of *eis).* The solution to reconciling Acts 2:38 with the rest of Scripture lies in seeing that *for,* both in Greek and English, can mean "because of." Peter is saying, "Repent! Then be baptized **because** your sins have been forgiven!" Rather than telling them to be baptized so that they could obtain forgiveness he is telling them to be baptized because of a forgiveness that comes about through repentance.

Interpreters have a choice with Acts 2:38. They can either stubbornly understand the verse in isolation and contradiction to the rest of Scripture, or they can adopt another legitimate (but admittedly more rare) meaning for the word *for.* The latter choice is obviously correct since it harmonizes Scripture keeping intact the principle of faith alone.[9]

Rom. 6:3-4

- Or do you not know that all of us who have been baptized into Christ Jesus have been baptized into His death? Therefore, we have been buried with Him through baptism into death, in order that as Christ was raised from

---

[9] The reader can, of course, find other interpretations of Acts 2:38 which also explain Peter's statement in ways not involving baptismal regeneration.

the dead through the glory of the Father, so
we too might walk in newness of life.

Confusion over this text can arise if one is ignorant of the doctrine of Spirit baptism. John the Baptist
kept predicting that Christ would baptize with the
Spirit as opposed to baptizing with water (Matt. 3:11;
Mark 1:8; Luke 3:16; John 1:33). As the book of Acts
begins, Christ tells His followers to wait for this
Spirit baptism (Acts 1:5), and it is from Peter's
statements in Acts 11:15-16 that one knows the first
such baptism of the Spirit took place on Pentecost
(Acts 2). Paul explains that the placing of a person
into Christ takes place by a Spirit baptism (1 Cor.
12:13). Since he uses the word *all* and since Spirit
baptism occurs at the time of union with Christ, it is
evident that every believer is baptized with the Holy
Spirit at the time of salvation, i.e., at the time of **faith**
in Christ as Savior. This Spirit baptism causes a union with Christ and all the benefits of Christ's death
and resurrection. It also causes a union with all other
believers who are also "in Christ." When Paul says in
Eph. 4:5 there is "one baptism," he probably refers to
the reality of "Spirit baptism" which makes a person
a Christian, as opposed to the symbol, i.e., "water
baptism." It is unquestionable that Scripture places
more importance upon Spirit baptism than water
baptism. The doctrine of Spirit baptism is fully considered in *Not By Bread Alone: An Outlined Guide to
Bible Doctrine*. It is sufficient at this point to note
that the Scripture knows of more than just water baptism and that Spirit baptism is the more important of

the two. Spirit baptism is the reality of which water baptism is the symbol.

There are several choices for dealing with Romans 6:3-4. First, one can interpret the text as requiring baptism for salvation. This interpretation makes the Scriptures inconsistent with one other. The second option is to take baptism as referring to Spirit baptism. This not only harmonizes Scripture, it also meshes with what is known of Spirit baptism. Paul taught in 1 Cor. 12:13 that Spirit baptism unites a believer with Christ. Probably, Rom. 6:3-4 is teaching about a type of baptism that unites a believer with Christ's death and resurrection life. Rom. 6:3-4 should probably be linked with Spirit baptism rather than with water baptism.[10]

---

[10] Though the author prefers to take baptism in Rom. 6:3-4 as Spirit baptism, one could understand Paul to mean water baptism without the inference that water baptism is a requirement for salvation. Baptism is to a believer what a wedding ring is to a married man or woman. It is the symbol of a relationship. It is possible to wear a ring and not be married (just as one could be baptized but not be a believer). It is also possible to be married without wearing a ring (just as one could be saved without ever being baptized). However, wedding rings for practical purposes do indicate marriage. The Apostle Paul probably could not imagine anyone in his day being baptized without faith. Since being a Christian might result in persecution, only those with genuine faith wanted water baptism. Neither could Paul imagine a believer rejecting water baptism. (There is seldom any valid reason for a believer refusing baptism today either.) To Paul there was no such thing as a baptized unbeliever or an unbaptized believer. Therefore, baptism was actually even a surer sign of **faith** than a wedding ring is of a marriage. If Rom. 6:3-4 is not taken as a reference to Spirit baptism, Paul could be understood to mean that **water baptism, as practiced in the New Testament**

Col. 2:11-12

- And in Him you were also circumcised with
  a circumcision made without hands, in the
  removal of the body of the flesh by the circumcision of Christ; having been buried with
  Him in baptism, in which you were also
  raised up with Him through faith in the
  working of God, who raised Him from the
  dead.

The Bible speaks of a spiritual circumcision just
as it does Spirit baptism. (See Deut. 10:16; 30:6; Jer.
4:4; 9:25-26; Ezek. 44:7-9; Rom. 2:26-29; and Phil.
3:3). "Spiritual circumcision" is a figure of speech
that refers to the removal of the flesh's inevitable
control over a believer's life. Rom. 6:3-4 teaches that
the believer shares in Christ's resurrection life by
Spirit baptism. Then it goes on to discuss the removal
of the flesh's inevitable control over the believer.
Death means separation. Since we died with Christ
by Spirit baptism, there has been a separation of "the
body of sin's" inevitable control (Rom. 6:6ff.).

It is evident that Paul is referring in Col. 2:11 to
spiritual circumcision, not literal circumcision. How
much clearer could he make it than to say: "a circumcision made without hands"? Furthermore, it is also
evident that the teachings of Romans 6 and Colossians 2 are parallel. Believers have been united with

---

**Church during conditions of persecution, was a certain evi-
dence of faith**. It is the faith symbolized by baptism that saves.
Romans 6 would be teaching the faith that inevitably results in
baptism (faith evidenced by baptism) causes a sharing in the
benefit of Christ's death, burial, and resurrection.

Christ and have died with Him. Death means separation, not the cessation of existence. Therefore, believers are dead to "the body of flesh" not in the sense of sin ceasing to exist, but in the sense of its dominion being removed, separated from us. This is spiritual circumcision. Finally, it ought to be evident that the union with Christ and benefits coming from it are based in Spirit baptism rather than water baptism. Colossians 2 is teaching the same thing as Romans 6 (although with varying terminology). Those who have been united with Christ by Spirit baptism have undergone what Paul calls a spiritual "circumcision" in Colossians 2 and "death to sin" in Romans 6. Both images refer to a removal or separation of sin's control.

The only explanation that can be given for taking Col. 2:11-12 to teach that baptism saves is theological bias. If one wants to maintain a system, he interprets texts in support of it (even if the result contradicts the rest of the Bible). Clearly one superior view of Col. 2:11-12 is that it refers to Spirit baptism instead of water baptism. With this view there is harmony with the rest of Scriptures teaching salvation by *faith alone*, there is a clear parallel with Romans 6, and there is not any basis for baptismal regeneration. An acceptable alternative would be to take baptism in Col. 2:12 to mean water baptism without thinking that baptism is a requirement for salvation. Paul would be assuming that water baptism is the certain token of faith. Faith as symbolized by baptism would be the real basis for sharing in the benefits of Christ's death and resurrection. Faith as displayed by baptism would be the basis for the separation of filth's control over the life, i.e., spiritual circumcision. (See footnote 10 for a parallel interpretation of Romans 6.)

1 Pet. 3:21

- Which [water] even you as a figure now saves, i.e., baptism (not of the flesh putting away of filth but for a good conscience an appeal unto God) through the resurrection of Jesus Christ.

This literal translation of the verse in approximate Greek word order shows that it is a difficult, obscure statement. Doctrine must be built upon clear and repeated texts. Furthermore, easy statements must help in the interpretation of difficult ones. To insist that 1 Pet. 3:21 can overturn the teaching of over 150 clear verses is quite obstinate.

First, notice that in the context, Peter is comparing the waters of baptism to the waters of Noah's flood. Water did not save Noah. The ark did. The ark saved Noah, and Noah went through the floodwaters. The waters of the flood remind Peter of the waters of baptism. To the early church there was no such thing as an unbaptized believer. Baptism inevitably and properly followed genuine faith in Christ. Peter's comparison seems to be something like this, "Just as Noah was saved by the ark and passed through the waters, you have been saved by Christ and have passed through the waters." A comparison can be drawn involving the salvation of Noah through floodwaters and the salvation of believers through baptismal waters without resorting to making 1 Pet. 3:21 imply baptismal regeneration.

Next it must be emphasized that Peter does not have to be interpreted as saying that baptism saves. It is equally valid to take Peter as saying baptism saves in a **figurative sense**. If the parentheses are dropped, the figurative sense in which baptism saves is associated with Christ's resurrection. Baptism symbolizes a union with Christ in His death and resurrection. Coming up from the water symbolized a sharing in Christ's new life, the resurrection. The reality behind this figure does indeed save. By Spirit baptism a believer is united to share in the benefits of Christ's death and to share in His resurrection life. Water baptism symbolizes this sharing of Christ's resurrection life. Thus, Peter can say baptism saves in a figure.

Finally, notice Peter adds parenthetical material so that his readers will not think he is teaching baptismal regeneration. He qualifies what he means by saying baptism saves. It is not the literal washing of the body's filth that causes salvation. It is rather the appeal to God for the cleansing of the heart that has both brought salvation and rendered the sinner a qualified candidate for water baptism. The cleansing of the flesh by a ritual is utterly worthless to save. However, the candidate's appeal unto God to be cleansed from sin through the blood of Christ is the basis both for salvation and legitimate water baptism.

1 Pet. 3:21 teaches that water baptism saves only in the figurative sense of symbolizing a sharing in Christ's life that came about by faith. Also, the only

element pertaining to water baptism that actually saves is the appeal to God for cleansing (by faith in Christ) that makes a person qualified to be baptized. There is absolutely no warrant in taking 1 Pet. 3:21 to deny salvation by faith alone and teach baptismal regeneration.

The Baptism of John and Salvation

Most Bible teachers correctly make a distinction between John's baptism and Christian baptism. John the Baptist's baptism was preparatory and future looking. Its goal was for people to prepare to welcome the King. Christian baptism is oriented to the past. It symbolizes identification with Christ's death, burial, and resurrection (Rom. 6:3-4 by application). Christ instituted Christian baptism when He gave the great commission (Matt. 28:18-20). Obviously, a ritual that symbolizes Christ's death and resurrection would not be instituted before the crucifixion and resurrection. John's baptism must be different than Christian baptism.

Since the rejection of the King, John the Baptist's baptism is no longer being practiced. Even many who believe that baptism is essential for salvation would not look to texts concerning John the Baptist to establish their error. However, because such texts could bring confusion they will be studied in this section.

- "As for me, I baptize you with water for repentance..." [Matt. 3:11].

- And all the country of Judea was going out to him, and all the people of Jerusalem; and they were being baptized by him in the Jordan River, confessing their sins [Mark 1:5].

- And he came into all the district around the Jordan, preaching a baptism of repentance for the forgiveness of sins [Luke 3:3].

The call to "prepare ye the way of the Lord" teaches that John's work was basically preparatory. He himself was not technically bringing or offering forgiveness of sins. He was directly attesting to One who could and would offer such forgiveness upon His arrival. He was calling people "to repent," i.e., to change their minds. The people of Judea especially needed to change their minds about the Messiah and His soon coming. They needed to be mentally changed and prepared to accept the King. The line "baptism of repentance for the forgiveness of sins" need not be taken to mean the people automatically were saved on the basis of John's baptism. The word *for* can mean "with a view to." (Mark is working for a graduation next year, i.e., with a view to graduation next year). John the Baptist was telling people to repent (change their thinking about the Messiah's coming) and be baptized with a view to obtaining forgiveness of sins that the Messiah would bring upon His arrival. The above verses do not conclusively teach that all who submitted to John's work were saved at the time of baptism. If one professed to be mentally prepared and willing to accept the king and was baptized by John upon this basis, he still had to accept the King after his arrival in order to have salvation and forgiveness. John's message and baptism prepared a person to accept the King with a view to a forgiveness of sins, which the King would pro-

vide when He arrived. The promised forgiveness of
sins did not happen unless the King was indeed accepted when He did come to Israel. Likely, some
whom John baptized later rejected Jesus' messianic
claim, and, the fact that they had been baptized would
not, in itself, save them. (See previous comments of
John 3:5.) The above texts can be paraphrased as
follows:

- "I baptize you with water because of repentance" (i.e., because of a change on thinking
  that is prepared to accept the coming King)
  [Matt 3:11].[11]

- John the Baptist appeared in the wilderness
  preaching a baptism based upon repentance
  with a view to a forgiveness of sins that the
  King would bring [Mark 1:4].

- And he came into all the district of Jordan,
  preaching a baptism based upon repentance
  (i.e., a changed mind about the coming Messiah) with a view to a forgiveness of sins that
  the King would bring [Luke 3:3].

It is best to view John's work as totally preparatory. He himself was not offering forgiveness of sins
to the people. He called for people to be mentally and
morally changed and prepared to accept One who

---

[11] Matt. 3:11 could also be translated: "I baptize you in water
with a view to repentance." It would have to be understood that
repentance was a prior condition to John's baptism but, also, that
baptism was intended to produce still more repentance. Such a
translation would make a nice parallel to 1 Cor. 12:13: (John
baptized in water with a view to repentance; Christ baptizes in
the Holy Spirit with a view to union in one body).

would grant such forgiveness when He came. John's baptism symbolized a readiness to accept the future King and His future forgiveness. John's baptism related to salvation by preparing people to accept the Savior. However, the promised forgiveness of sin had to await the King's arrival. John prepared for salvation by baptism. Christ provided salvation by **faith alone**.

If one should still insist that John's ministry actually provided forgiveness, as opposed to preparing for a future forgiveness that Christ would offer, then one could contend that such a forgiveness must have been based upon repentance, not baptism.

If John actually offered forgiveness of sins, it was based upon repentance, not baptism. Yet, there is every reason to believe John was not himself offering forgiveness. His baptism symbolized a preparation to receive a future forgiveness of sins that the Messiah would bring. Finally, John's baptism is not even being practiced since the rejection of the King. Therefore, there is no basis for using texts relative to John the Baptist's baptism as evidence that baptism is a condition for salvation.

Confess Jesus Before Men to be Saved.

The practice of giving an invitation to walk an aisle in order to trust in Christ is neither Scriptural nor unscriptural. It is neither commanded nor forbidden. Churches will vary in opinions as to the wisdom of this evangelistic method. However, there is a dan-

ger of creating a major error in order to pressure people into "coming forward."

The Scriptures base salvation upon faith alone. If
one adds "a public confession of Jesus" to the sole
condition of faith, he is preaching "another gospel"!
The addition of "public confession of Jesus" as a requirement for salvation is often done with an "end-
justifies-the-means" attitude. It can also arise out of
sheer ignorance, sloppy habits, the desire to count
numbers of conversions, or the uncritical acceptance
of tradition without consideration of its Scriptural
foundation. By telling people they must publicly confess to be saved, speakers create pressure to get "de-
cisions." However, consider the poor timid soul who
has no trouble deciding he should trust in Christ but
not enough courage to decide to step forward in a
crowded church. For such, the speaker has given a
man-made and erroneous condition for salvation. It is
an artificial barrier to salvation that is contrary to
God's Word and should not be accepted by the
church. Isn't it possible to believe in Christ in settings where public confession is not possible such as
a motel room with a Gideon Bible or a quiet bedroom
with mother? Would it not also be possible to make a
public profession without having real faith? The most
commonly abused text used to show that public confession is required for salvation is Rom. 10:9-10a.[12]

---

[12] Obviously, none of the contexts of the verses under consideration refer to the practice of a public altar call. Furthermore, few
people would want to take this view to its logical outcome and
base salvation upon witnessing. This would end in a works based

Rom. 10:9-10

- ...that if you confess with your mouth Jesus as Lord, and believe in your heart that God raised Him from the dead, you shall be saved; for with the heart man believes, resulting in righteousness, and with the mouth he confesses, resulting in salvation.

In Rom. 10:9-10 Paul is giving an example of his method for Jewish evangelism. (See Rom. 10:1.) He says that the method he uses involves confessing with the mouth the Lord Jesus and believing in the heart that God raised Him from the dead. As a good Bible expositor, Paul proves that his evangelistic method is valid by supporting it with Scripture. The context following v. 10 proves from the Old Testament that Paul is correct to ask for belief and confession. Verse 11 proves that his appeal to believe in the resurrection is valid: "For [because] the Scriptures say [in Isa. 28:16] whoever believes in Him will not be disappointed." Then in v. 13 Paul gives Scriptural proof for his appeal to confess that Jesus is Lord (i.e., God, Messiah, Master). Quoting Joel 2:32, v. 13 says, "For [because] whoever will call on the name of the Lord will be saved." In condensed version Paul's argument runs like this: "I asked the Jews to believe in the resurrected Lord because Isa. 28:16 asks for belief, and I ask for confession because Joel 2:32 gives the invitation to call upon the Lord for salvation." Notice carefully that v. 13 defines the type of confession Paul

---

system parallel to the Jehovah's Witnesses' concept that salvation comes through working at witnessing.

wanted. He urged people to "confess" in the sense of
"calling upon the Name of the Lord." **The confession
Paul wanted is made in a prayer to God. He is not
thinking of a confession made before humans**.
Confess in Romans 10:9 equals calling upon God in
prayer and acknowledging to Him that Jesus is the
Lord in Rom. 10:13. The argument of this text makes
it clear the confession of which v. 9 speaks is expressed by calling upon the name of the Lord (as in
vv. 12-13). **Paul is not asking his fellow Jews to
give a confession of faith before men in order to
obtain salvation. He is asking them to confess that
Jesus Christ is their Lord (Messiah) in a prayer to
God.** Acknowledging that Jesus Christ is the Son of
God is an essential part of saving faith. One good
Scripturally-approved method of expressing this acknowledgment is through a prayer to God. However,
Rom. 10:9-10 has nothing to do with a confession
made to other people either in public or private.

Matt. 10:32-33 and Luke 12:8-9

- "Everyone therefore who shall confess Me
  before men, I will also confess him before
  My Father, who is in heaven. But whosoever
  shall deny Me before men, I will also deny
  him before My Father who is in heaven"
  [Matt. 10:32-33].

- "And I say to you, everyone who confesses Me before men, the Son of Man shall
  confess him also before the angels of God;
  but he who denies Me before men shall be
  denied before the angels of God" [Luke 12:8-
  9].

Matthew 10:32ff. and Luke 12:8ff. are also texts that have been used to establish that public confession of Jesus is a requirement to salvation. When viewed in isolation from the rest of Scripture, these texts could be so interpreted. However, the result would be a contradiction with over 150 texts that condition salvation upon faith alone.

If the Lord's statements can also be viewed in a way that harmonizes them with the rest of Scripture, then not only will the *faith alone* position be maintained but so will Biblical infallibility. It is not of ultimate importance which of the following views of Matt. 10:32 and Luke 12:8 is the correct one. The important concern is that there are interpretations that do harmonize all the Scriptures and preserve both Biblical infallibility and *sola fide* (faith alone). **Any** of these interpretations are preferable to taking these two texts to make a contradiction in Scripture. The possibilities will now be discussed.

Apostolic View

One way of reconciling Matt. 10:32 and Luke 12:8-9 with the 150 plus verses that teach *faith alone* is to interpret and apply them strictly to the persons to whom the words were spoken. They are parallel texts given **primarily to the apostles** (Matt. 10:1-2; Luke 12:1 "to His disciples first...") who were announcing the Kingdom (Matt. 10:7) to Israel only (Matt. 10:6). If the warning is restricted to the twelve, then the emphasis upon acknowledging Christ by confessing or denying Him may have been for the benefit of Judas Iscariot. Perhaps it is true of the twelve that those who confessed Christ will be honored in heaven, but those who denied (Judas) will be denied by Christ before the Father in heaven. By restricting these statements to the specific persons being addressed, they can be handled in a way that does not contradict *sola fide*.[13]

Tribulation View

There is also precedent for Christ viewing the apostles as representatives of tribulation saints. Apparently, Christ considered the tribulation saints as extensions of the apostolic work, and He could view the connection rather directly without the intervening church system. This occurs in Luke 21 where Christ's discourse about Jerusalem's destruction in apostolic times ends up merging with the conflicts in the end times. The Lord speaks to His apostles as though they were the ones who would experience tribulation anguish in the end times. In the Matt. 10:32-33 context this same process occurs. In Matt. 10:6 Christ tells the apostles to go **only to Israel**, but, before the lecture is over, Christ seems to view the apostles as representatives of the tribulation saints. He says they will be dragged before rulers and **Gentiles** to give witness (Matt. 10:18). In language paralleling the tribulation account of Matt. 24:9 and 13, Christ tells them they will be hated by all (Matt. 10:22) and will be delivered from this time of trouble by endurance

---

[13] The context of Matthew 10 would give stronger support to restricting these comments to the apostles than does the context of Luke 12. The Lord speaks to "His disciples first" though the multitude listened (Luke 12:1).

to the end (Matt. 10:22). Matt. 10:23 is the most explicitly tribulational. It says the persecuted witnesses would not get to all the cities in Israel "until the **Son of Man comes**."

It is possible to view Christ's words in Matt. 10:32-33 as also having a dual reference to both the apostles and tribulation saints. This allows for interesting possibilities in the reconciliation of the texts with the *faith alone* doctrine taught elsewhere in Scripture. During the tribulation period believers will be forced to either identify with Christ or against Him by the acceptance or rejection of the mark of the beast, i.e., Antichrist (see Rev. 13:16-17). The only God-imposed condition for salvation is faith. Yet, conditions will be such in the tribulation time that a Satanic-engendered requirement to being a believer will be a public confession of Christ by refusal of the mark (Rev. 20:4). All who do not believe in Christ will deny Him by the same mark. God requires only faith to be saved, but the devil's system will require a refusal of the mark to be a believer. Thus, the result is that **all believers in the Tribulation will publicly confess Christ and all unbelievers in the Tribulation will deny Him.**

If the interpreter restricts the words of Matt. 10:32-33 and Luke 12:8-9 strictly to the apostles and the Tribulation generation, the resulting interpretation harmonizes with *sola fide*. God's only condition for salvation is faith. Yet, with the twelve and with the religious in the Tribulation (viewed as an extension of apostolic work), conditions on earth will be such as to force these groups to either confess or deny

Christ in a **definitive and irrevocable way**. While applications may be drawn for other groups of God's people (including those, in our time, under pressure to deny Christ), no other groups will face the same absolute pressure to confess or deny Christ in such an irrevocable sense. These verses teach us by application that a believer, in the present time, should never deny Christ. However, present embarrassment about being a Christian is not the same as publicly betraying the Messiah to death (Judas) or selling one's soul to the Antichrist. If the statements of Matt. 10:32-33 and Luke 12:8-9 are restricted to the special conditions facing the apostles and the tribulation generation, then they can be harmonized with the truth that faith in Christ is God's only requirement for salvation. Those with a dispensational view of Scripture will more readily adopt this possible means of reconciling Matt.10:32-33 and Luke 12:8-9 with the *faith alone* position. There is nothing unusual about a truth referring to the apostles or to tribulation saints but not directly referring to the church. However, it is possible to understand Matt. 10:32-33 and Luke 12: 8-9 in additional ways that leave it both unrestricted and yet compatible with the *faith alone* doctrine.[14]

---

[14] One problem with the apostolic view is that Peter did deny the Lord in a limited sense while Judas confessed Jesus for a number of years. If we restrict Matthew 10 and Luke 12 to the apostles, then Jesus must be talking about apostolic descriptions that accurately reveal beliefs. In Peter's case, he customarily confessed Jesus when viewed as a trend over a lifetime (though he had occasional lapses). In Judas' case, he confessed Jesus for a while but denied Him to a degree that proved he lacked faith. All interpretations of Matthew 10 and Luke 12 must include the fact that

Rewards View

Perhaps Jesus speaks of future rewards rather than of salvation. Jesus might mean those who confess Him as a worthy Savior would be confessed as being worthy of rewards at the Judgment Seat. Those who deny the Lord as unworthy of acknowledgment here will not be acknowledged as worthy of full reward in heaven. Though Matt. 10:28 and Luke 12:5 refer to the soul's eternal destiny, it is preferable to view the overall text as referring to the rewards of a believer rather than to contradict salvation by faith alone. This view does have the advantage of being simple.

The "Either Extreme" View

Perhaps Jesus presupposes the words of confession or denial truly reveal a person's faith or lack of faith. We could limit the passage to definitions of confession and denial, which would be strictly consistent with salvation by faith. Confession would become virtually a synonym for believing. Denial means refusal to believe.

In the **extreme**, one who **always denies Christ** shows he is an unbeliever. On the other hand, a **believer** will confess Christ to others (at least to other believers) at some point in life. He or she **will not deny at all times** (like a typical unbeliever).

Thus, the interpreter might take for granted that the Lord speaks only of a type of confession to others

---

words do not always reveal the heart and that unbelievers have occasionally confessed while believers can occasionally deny. Even if we restrict the Lord's direct words to the apostles, we end up with a view similar to the "general description view".

based in faith or a type of denial to others based in
unbelief though the text has not given such explicit
restriction. The Lord's teaching could be paraphrased
to read: "Unbelievers display their rejection by constantly denying Me all their lives. **Those who deny**
and reject Me at **all times** prove they are **unsaved**. A
believer will at some time in life confess to others, at
least to other trustworthy Christians, that he knows
Me. A **believer** might deny occasionally but he **will
not deny always**. At some time and to someone he
will admit he has faith."

One who always denies is an unbeliever. One
who is a believer will acknowledge Christ some-
time.[15] The direct application to the original listeners
would be to confess Christ in settings involving pressure rather than just in calm, unpressured settings
involving trustworthy friends. Believers will confess
Jesus at least some of the time. They should be consistent during persecution and not act like typical unbelievers who always deny Christ. The context
clearly warns of persecution, (Matt. 10:28, 34-39) but
perhaps the confession or denial under view need not
only take place in a setting of persecution. [16]

---

[15] To use a sports analogy, a believer may not bat 1,000, but,
unlike a person who constantly denies Christ, a true believer will
not bat .000 either.

[16] Perhaps the reader can tell why the author calls this the "Either
Extreme View." A person who denies Christ at all times over a
lifespan reveals he has no faith. A believer will confess Jesus at
least minimally. He will confess to some people in some settings,
(maybe a private conversation or in the hospital room with a
pastor) that he believes. Because the unbeliever's denial would
have to be total while a believer's confession could be timid,

"Here" vs. "Hereafter" or the "Confession to God View"

The words of Matthew 10 and Luke 12 seem to contrast the "here" and the "hereafter", earth and heaven, now and eternity. Suppose we do not take the phrase *before men* to refer to a confession (or denial) made in the presence of others but rather understand it to mean something like "during your time among men." The Lord would be contrasting the present life among or before men on this earth with a future in heaven. Furthermore, if the **confession** under consideration **is made to the Father** (as in Rom. 10:9-10), then Jesus' teachings have been reconciled with the truth of salvation by faith alone. The resulting meaning would be this: "If you confess Me **to the Father** during your life before men, I will confess you **to the Father** in eternity before the angels. If you deny Me as Savior during your life before men, I will deny you to the Father in eternity before the angels." The contrasting destinies would be confession to the Father now in this life before men, or Christ's denial to the Father at a future time before angels.[17] If we under-

---

occasional, and minimal, the intensity of behavior would go in the opposite direction.

[17] The context refers to persecution. Persecution gives the opportunity to confess Christ to others or the temptation to deny Christ to others. Still Jesus might be thinking of a confession of faith **made to the Father** in Matt. 10:32-33 and Luke 12:8-9. He would be building upon a confession made to the Father as an example of how a believer should consistently confess Jesus in times of persecution. We should confess Jesus to others just as we have confessed Him to the Father.

stand the confession to be made to God and take the phrase *before men* to mean life on earth, there is no conflict with salvation by *faith alone*. Any of the above views is preferable to making public confession a condition for salvation. The author included them for consideration but prefers the last option.

General Description View

Believers usually (but not always) admit they know the Lord. Unbelievers usually (but not always) deny the Lord. If the preceding ways to reconcile Matthew 10 and Luke 12 with the doctrine of salvation by faith alone are unacceptable, the final attempt at explanation may satisfy because it is quite simple.

The Lord's words do **not** give a **condition of salvation** but rather a **general description** of most believers most of the time.[18] Most believers typically confess and admit they know Jesus as an **overall trend during their lifespans.** This is especially true if we include all types of situations rather than just

---

[18] Jesus employs a similar thought pattern in Matt. 25:31-46. The sheep who feed, clothe, and visit the Lord's brethren (technically the Jews in the tribulation period) do not earn salvation by these good works. Feeding, clothing, and visiting are **not conditions** for salvation but rather **descriptions** which reveal the person has faith. Only those with faith will minister to the Jews against the objection of the Antichrist. Salvation comes through faith, but those saved can be described as those who do good works. Faith is demonstrated by behavior. Likewise, in Matthew 10 and Luke 12 confession is not a condition for salvation but a description of the way a believer should and usually does act. Denial is the description of the way an unbeliever usually acts. A Christian who denies is not acting out the normal description of a believer but instead hypocritically acts like an unbeliever.

those involving intimidation or pressure (e.g., believers nearly always confess faith to other believers). Most unbelievers typically deny and will not acknowledge Jesus as an overall trend during their life span. Again, this is especially true in non-pressure situations involving other non-Christians. The Lord would neither be teaching that salvation is based upon confession or witnessing nor that salvation is lost by denials. His point would be that His disciples should be consistent to the typical and general behavior they will frequently exhibit throughout their lives. In time of threat or persecution they should not change from the normal behavior of most believers most of the time.

As a general and loose description, believers admit they believe. Unbelievers deny they believe. There may be individuals who are exceptions to the general rule. Furthermore, almost anyone is capable of occasional words inconsistent with their usual pattern. Still, as a basic tendency, believers acknowledge Christ, unbelievers do not. The Lord wants us to be consistent to the overall trend and general description of a Christian in situations when it would be easy to speak like an unbeliever. The general **description** view is another way to reconcile Matthew 10 and Luke 12 with a salvation **conditioned** upon faith alone. [19]

---

[19] Viewing the Lord's words as a loose and general description of believers (rather than a condition for salvation) has the advantage of taking other Scriptural teaching into consideration. The rest of the Bible teaches that believers can fail to admit to others that they have faith. Peter is the outstanding example (John 18:25),

Summary

Romans 10:9-10 is not discussing a public confession, but rather the confession associated with salvation is a private confession made to God. Rom. 10:9 should be equated with Rom. 10:12-13. Confession equals a calling on the name of the Lord to be saved.

Likewise, Matt. 10:32-33 and Luke 12:8-9 do not have to be interpreted as contradicting the 150 plus verses that give faith alone as a condition for salvation. One could restrict them as being directed either to the apostles alone or also to the tribulation saints who faced or will face special conditions unparalleled by any other groups. If one does not feel convinced

---

and John 12:42 also states there were Pharisees who believed but would not confess the Lord publicly because they feared Jewish authorities. Apparently, a believer can fail to confess Christ on occasions but still have an overall life described as a "confessor." He might admit to faith in safe situations with a pastor, other believers, or trusted family and friends. No doubt there are timid believers in Moslem countries in our time who would not dare make a public confession.

On the other hand, Judas' example and Matt. 7:21-23 show that an unbeliever might occasionally confess faith, but his overall description in life would be that of denial. So long as the confession made in Matthew 10 and Luke 12 is understood as being made to other people (not to God the Father), it will be necessary to understand the Lord's words as general and loose descriptions qualified by other Scriptures. Most believers usually admit the Savior. Most unbelievers usually deny Him. Keep in mind that the primary intent of Matthew 10 and Luke 12 concerns how believers should handle opposition. Soteriology is not the Lord's primary subject. Thus, He could be describing only the typical behavior of most believers (and unbelievers) without listing every detailed exception. He holds believers to the typical behavior of confessing Him even in times of persecution.

by the contexts that these verses are being directed to specialized groups, then the verses are still capable of interpretations that are compatible with faith alone. Maybe the subject is the gain or loss of rewards and not salvation (Rewards View). Maybe Christ meant a believer would confess Him to at least some degree while those who consistently deny are unbelievers (Either Extreme View). Another idea would be Christ taught that those who confess Him to the Father in this life before men would avoid denial to the Father in eternity before angels ("Here" vs. "Hereafter" View). Another suggestion would be that the Lord gives usual descriptions of how the saved act instead of conditions to be saved (General Description View). The resulting lessons for the original listeners from at least three of the options end up the same. The disciples had already confessed Jesus to God and would confess Him to others. He wanted them to be true to that confession in time of trouble.

It is not necessary to argue which of the above views is correct. The main point is that they are alternatives to thinking public confession is a condition for salvation in addition to faith.

Ask Jesus Into Your Heart to Be Saved

This phrase is often used to express a condition for salvation when dealing with children. It can be understood as an equivalent for receiving Jesus as Savior by faith. Therefore, many children have had the gospel communicated by this phrase and have genuinely trusted in Christ.

However, the line "ask Jesus into your heart" is also capable of great misunderstanding. It is even possible for a person to "ask Jesus into your heart" and be completely ignorant of the Savior's death and resurrection or of the idea of trust. Furthermore, Christ's entrance into the heart is a result of salvation rather than a condition for it. The Bible **never** uses such terminology in evangelism and it should be avoided.

The Greek word for heart is *kardia* from which cardiac is derived. It is used between 157-160 times depending upon which manuscripts are counted. The student may consult a concordance to satisfy his own mind that "asking Jesus into ones heart" is **never made a condition for salvation** in the Bible. To state the truth a different way, one could assert people are constantly being saved **without** asking Jesus into their hearts. It simply is not a condition for salvation. The Scriptures do say that one believes with his heart (Luke 24:25; Acts 15:9; Rom.10:9-10), but neither the Gospel of John, nor the evangelistic sermons in Acts, nor in the great theological treatise in Romans, nor anywhere in the New Testament is "asking Jesus into ones heart" made a condition for salvation. **One must not confuse a result of salvation with a requirement for salvation.**

It is possible that asking Jesus into ones heart is viewed as a condition for salvation because of a superficial interpretation of Rev. 3:20.

- "Behold, I stand at the door and knock; if anyone hears My voice and opens the door, I will come in to him, and will dine with him, and he with Me" [Rev. 3:20].

Notice that the word *heart* is not even used in Rev. 3:20. The interpreter also needs to realize that there is a space between the words "in" and "to." This verse is saying the Lord will come **in with** a person not **inside** or **into** a person. The Greek phrase in Rev. 3:20 (*eiserkomai*) is used eight other times in the New Testament, and it never means "inside of" (Mark 7:25; 15:43; Luke 1:28; Acts 10:3; 11:3; 16:40; 17:2; 28:8). In Mark 15:43 Joseph of Arimathea "went in [unto] Pilate and asked for the body of Jesus." He did not go inside of Pilate! He went "in with" or "in unto" Pilate. Likewise, Rev. 3:20 is teaching that Jesus is willing to come unto or "in with" a person to have fellowship with him. Christ's work of indwelling a person's heart is not in view in Rev. 3:20. No verse conditions salvation upon asking Jesus into one's heart.

Confess Sins to Obtain Salvation

The confession of sin is a very important Christian doctrine. However, it needs to be viewed in its proper place. Teachings about confession of sin are primarily directed to believers. In His role as Judge, God has already forgiven the believer of all sins (Col. 2:13). In His role as Father, God still can become angry and forgiveness will need to be obtained by the believer through confession (i.e., acknowledgment of sin). Thus, believers are urged to confess their sins to obtain forgiveness from the Father (cf. 1 John 1:9; 1 Cor. 11:31; Matt. 6:12). In its proper place the doctrine of confessing sins is most true and most vital.

However, the Scriptures do not give the confession of sins as a condition for salvation. True, a person who comes in faith to Christ is implicitly admitting his own sinfulness in a general sense, but this is different from a requirement of listing, naming, and confessing specific offenses in order to obtain salvation. The latter activity could actually be viewed as a work of penance with salvation being earned by the meritorious act of confessing sins. Consider the fact that a person could list and confess many, many sins without even a basic knowledge of the cross or faith in the person of Jesus Christ. Were not the monasteries of the Middle Ages full of poor wretches who confessed sin after sin but never trusted in Christ to forgive them? Also, consider the truth that nowhere is confession of specific sins made a requirement for salvation. Just as one could confess many sins without trusting in Christ, so also one can trust in Christ without confessing any sin specifically. It is sufficient that a person acknowledge **sinfulness** in a general sense and wants to have deliverance by trusting in Christ. Confession of specific sin is a proper means for a believer to obtain forgiveness from God in His role as Father. However, the means for a sinner to obtain forgiveness from God in His role as Judge is **faith alone**.

A few people use 1 John 1:9 to argue that specific confession of sin is a condition for a lost person to be saved. However, the context and phraseology show that the verse is directed to believers. In 1 John 2:1, John shows he is writing to "little children," i.e., believers. He writes to those for whom Jesus Christ is an Advocate or Comforter. In 1 John 2:2, John distinguished between his readers and the world. It is easy to establish that 1 John 1:9 is directed to believers rather than to unbelievers. The confession of specific sins is not a Biblical condition for salvation. God in His role as Judge forgives sin on the basis of faith in Christ. If a person has genuinely placed his faith in Christ, he has already acknowledged his sin to a degree that is sufficient for salvation.

Forgive Others in Order to be Saved

A large church listed "freely forgive as Christ has forgiven you" as a condition for salvation in one of its advertisements for a "revival meeting." The ad specifically said this is one of God's "terms" for salvation. There is no question that the Bible encourages forgiveness, but there are great problems with saying the Bible teaches forgiveness of others as a condition for salvation. First, in the truest sense it is impossible for one who does not know Christ to forgive as Christ does. One must first be saved and experience God's forgiveness in order to truly forgive others. Requiring forgiveness of all others before salvation occurs places an insurmountable barrier upon a person who may want to be forgiven by God but cannot bring himself to forgive those who have victimized him. In fact, even God does not forgive all sins committed against Him! Christians should forgive easily, but if the offense is too great, even a Christian is not required to forgive after all attempts to reconcile have failed. (See Matt. 18:15-17.) If Christians and even God Himself do not always forgive, it is absurd to make complete forgiveness of others a condition for the lost to meet in order to obtain salvation. Second, requiring forgiveness conditions salvation upon something a person does as opposed to an acceptance of what Christ has done. It adds work to a pure faith that accepts God's pure grace. Third, even if a hypothetical forgiveness of all others could take place, the person would still be lost in sins. If a natural man could completely forgive others, he still would be unsaved until he learns about and trusts in Christ and His work on the cross. Finally, there is no Scripture whatsoever to support the idea that God demands a person forgive everyone of all things before he can be saved.

Matt. 6:14-15 could be misinterpreted to teach "forgiving others" as a condition for salvation. However, Christ is addressing those who are already saved (v. 9, "…Our Father who art in heaven…"). He is teaching that those believers who hold unforgiving grudges against others will not obtain forgiveness from God in His role as Father. God has already forgiven believers in His role as Judge by virtue of faith in Christ. Yet, if a believer absolutely refuses to forgive another who requests it, that believer will in turn remain unforgiven in the sense that he is not in fellowship with God. Fellowship with God the Father is conditioned upon forgiving those who sincerely request it. However, salvation is conditioned upon faith alone.

Deny Self and Forsake All to be Saved

There are several passages where Christ commands complete dedication to Himself. No one will argue the point that Christ requires a complete allegiance and denial of self. However, it is debatable that He requires complete denial of self in order to obtain salvation. There is a distinction between what God requires after salvation and what He requires for salvation.

Before texts that call for self-denial are examined, it will be conceded that they could be interpreted to require utmost sacrifice, self-denial, and obedience to earn salvation. However, they also can be interpreted to harmonize with the clearly Biblical position that salvation is by grace through faith. There is nothing unusual about a teaching that can be taken in more than one sense in isolation from the rest of Scripture. However, logic and the authority of Scripture demand that any interpretation that eliminates contradictions be preferred. Christ told the rich young ruler to give all that he possessed to the poor and to follow Him (Matt. 19:21-22). Isolated from other Scriptures, this text is capable of teaching that salvation is earned by sacrificial giving. However, it could also be understood that salvation would come by following Christ. Because the man's wealth prevented him from following Christ, it was in his individual case essential that he relinquish that wealth in order to become a believer. Thus, his salvation was to be by faith alone rather than by charitable deeds, but Christ wanted him to remove the barrier that money caused so that he could became a believer. The text itself is capable of both interpretations. However, the correct one is the latter because it harmonizes with the rest of Scripture.

Luke 9:23-26

(See also Matt. 16:24-28 and Mark 8:34-38)

- And He was saying to them all, "If anyone wishes to come after Me, let him deny himself, and take up his cross daily, and follow Me. For whoever wishes to save his life shall lose it, but whoever loses his life for My sake, he is the one who will save it. For what is a man profited if he gains the whole world, and loses or forfeits himself? For whoever is ashamed of Me and My words, of him will the Son of Man be ashamed when He comes in His glory, and the glory of the Father and of the holy angels."

To whom does Jesus address these words? Are those listening believers, unbelievers, or a mixture? The context in Luke 9:18 speaks of the disciples (see also Matt. 16:24), but verse 23 uses the word *all*. Mark 8:34 says, "and He summoned the multitude with His disciples." The disciples (apostles) are believers, but many in the crowd are unbelievers. It would not be unusual, then or now, to deliver a sermon to a mixed audience. While Jesus is getting believers ready for persecution, many unsaved listened to the conversation. The best way to explain this passage is to study what the Lord's teaching in Luke 9:23-26 meant for unbelievers and then to consider what He intended for believers. First, let's be clear on what this passage does **not** teach.

Misunderstandings

Luke 9:23-26 cannot mean salvation comes through self-denial, constant sacrifice, and intense effort. The pursuit of salvation would be a daily process. Either one is never sure when one has done enough to deserve salvation or one must keep striving to retain salvation. Every day would be a new test.

If we were to follow a similar approach to vv. 24-25, then salvation would come through martyrdom, but then few would be saved. The resulting theology would be like false religions, which promise heaven to fanatics who die for their cause. One could also take vv. 24-25 to require the loss of control (authority) over one's own life. Then salvation would be earned by giving the control of life over to Jesus. This theology does not bother some zealous and unthinking evangelists, but all the above ideas contradict the more than 150 verses which teach salvation through faith alone.

Meaning for Unbelievers:
"Believe whatever the cost."

In Luke 9:23 the Lord calls listeners to follow Him without limits. However, many in the crowd had not even begun the process of following. For them the most pressing application would be to take the first step. They had to begin following the Lord with the first step: salvation by faith.

To unbelievers, Luke 9:23 primarily means that if social conditions are such that a person must suffer and take risks in order to become a believer, then he must still believe. Salvation cannot be earned by self-denial, enduring persecution, or accepting risks. However, if placing faith in Christ involves danger, being ridiculed, or leads to pain, then that price must be paid in order to become a believer. Faith alone saves. God the Judge will not accept the excuse; "I could not trust Jesus because doing so would have meant rejection, persecution, or possible martyrdom."

Luke 9:24a warns that those so intimidated by fear that they refuse to believe in Jesus might save their physical lives but would lose eternal life. The seemingly safe decision to reject Jesus preserves this life at the peril of eternal death.

Not only can potential hardship, ridicule, or death block faith, but also the world might reward those who turn away from following Christ in initial saving faith. When a person yields to pressures not to accept Jesus in faith, he will often find acceptance by the unsaved world system. He may even be blessed and exalted by the world.

Jesus warns unbelievers in the multitude not to choose the superficial benefits of rejecting Him to gain the world's acceptance. They might gain socially; however, they will lose genuine life. They forfeit self. They can either choose to put their lives in mortal jeopardy by faith in Christ, or they can place their souls in eternal jeopardy by safely, comfortably, and perhaps profitably rejecting Him as Savior.

The type of shame in view in verse 26 is a shame that causes one to turn away in unbelief from the Lord. If one is so ashamed of Christ that he rejects Him as Savior, then Christ will reject him in the end.

If shame leads a person to unbelief now, the Lord will be too embarrassed and ashamed of that person to have an eternal relationship. To unbelievers, Jesus' words in Luke 9:23 mean they must overcome any fears or allurements from the world and trust Him. Though the call in verse 23 is to follow completely, they must begin to follow by believing in the Lord Jesus. Safety and even gain are a poor trade for eternal death.

The Lord's words warn unbelievers to begin following Jesus whatever it costs. However, His teachings also have meaning for the disciples (apostles) who are already saved. What was the Lord teaching them? How shall we apply the Lord's ideas to believers today?

Meaning for Believers:

"Don't act like them now....the world
can persecute but cannot
take your eternal life."

Jesus had told the disciples in Luke 9:22 that rejection and suffering was on its way. Though they had already ignored the risks, and had accepted the dangers and threats associated with becoming believers, they still faced pressures not unlike those faced with the risks of initial faith in Christ. Yes, they had chosen the first step. In faith they had begun the process of following, but the choice to follow Christ to a further degree in the face of trouble would have to be made repeatedly through life. Constant danger and hardship was ahead. Risks did not end with faith. The choice to ignore the threats and the temptations to

gain by not following would have to be made per-
petually. Just as the world pressures the unsaved to
not take the first step (faith) in following Jesus, the
world threatens conflict and uses enticements to hin-
der believers from unlimited following. The disciples
had not been pushed away from starting to follow
Jesus, but would they be stopped from a complete
following of Jesus in the critical and high-pressure
days to come?

Except for a brief phrase (about martyrdom at the
close of Luke 9:24), vv. 24-26 probably refer to unbelievers.[20] Still, these truths about unbelievers apply
to the disciples. Believers can learn from those who
choose safety and comfort over faith in Christ. Such
are extremely negative examples of how not to think.
What does their choice of safety and gain over following Christ in even the first step of faith teach believers who should follow completely?

In v. 24 the Lord uses a *reductio ad absurdum*
method (reduction to the absurd) to show the disciples they should not allow the world's opposition to
limit how much they would follow Christ. Taken to
its extreme, those who wish to save their lives will
not even trust Christ. They avoid ridicule. They avoid

---

[20] If one wishes to take Luke 9:23ff. as addressed to **only believers**, then *shame* in v. 26 could refer to loss of rewards. The *saving* of life in vv. 24-25 would likely include *saving* this life from
wasting its potential for God. However, references to *all* (Luke
9:23) and the *multitude* (Mark 8:34) coupled with warnings about
the loss of a soul (Matt. 16:26; Mark 8:36) seem to favor that the
Lord spoke to a mixed audience with different applications intended for the disciples and the lost.

the cross and any personal cross. They also lose eternal life. They gain from the world. They forfeit themselves eternally. The disciples had not totally agreed with such logic, or they would not have taken the first step in following, i.e., faith in Christ. They had begun rejecting fearful thinking when they believed. Should they return to a cowardly, worldly, and selfish mindset now and choose to limit how far they would follow? They had taken risks to begin following Christ; should they now lose courage? The unsaved lose ultimate values by such reasoning. Though the disciples already possess eternal life, nothing good would come from thinking and acting like unbelievers. They had taken risks to start following. They should now choose to follow completely.

The first part of Luke 9:24 describes unbelievers who choose preservation of this life over faith in Christ. The last part of Luke 9:24 describes the disciples. They had already ignored any consequences of becoming believers. If that decision to start following the Lord in faith (and future decisions/actions consistently arising from continuing to follow) should cost their lives for Christ's sake, they would still have eternal life. Eternal life is not earned on the merit of suffering martyrdom. Eternal life came when the disciples risked in order to believe. Should any part of following Christ (whether the first step in faith or continued following in obedience) risk physical life, then the believer still has encouragement from his assurance of eternal life.[21] From an eternal view the world can inflict no harm. No persecution can kill eternal life.

Jesus reassures His disciples they had made the right choice by refusing to play it safe. Just as they had risked life in order to take the first step of faith, they should continue to follow now whatever the danger or cost. Whatever drawbacks may come from following Christ (beginning to follow or continuing to follow) are worth the price. Those who have disregarded any possible hardship to start following Jesus should not act like cowardly unbelievers by limiting how far they will follow after salvation. No good comes from the decision to choose safety, comfort, and profit over trusting in the Lord Jesus. No good can arise from choosing these same things over following in continued dedication. Following fully saves from losing this life in the sense of wasting it and saves from forfeiting the full potential of this life (vv. 24-25 interpreted not as restricted to martyrdom only, but also as wasting life's potential). By implication, Luke 9:26 means the Master will be righteously proud (opposite of ashamed) of committed disciples who follow without limits. Luke 9:27 and the fol-

---

[21] Efforts to continue following after taking the initial step of faith can be seen as ultimately rooted in the original choice to trust Christ. If there had been no faith, there would not be any danger from persecution caused by ongoing obedient behaviors. Continuing to follow consistently arises from beginning the process in faith. In this extended sense, the disciple risked death for his fundamental decision to trust Christ in the past (though it would be acts of subsequent obedience in keeping with that original faith which actually would trigger even greater danger).

lowing account of the transfiguration remind us that, to the degree we follow now, we will share in the Lord's glory in eternity.

Luke 9:23-26 and its parallels can definitely be interpreted compatibly with salvation by faith alone. For unbelievers, it simply means to accept whatever price must be paid in order to initiate following by trusting in Christ. For believers, the passage means to continue to follow regardless of the pressures or temptations to stop along the way. Jesus calls believers to follow even further by pointing to the tragic choice of those who favor total safety in this life by refusing to trust in the Savior. Their disastrous example shows believers not to adopt the same cowardly behavior when it comes to following completely. Christians must be careful how they use ideas like self-denial, forsaking, and suffering in evangelistic settings. They have validity only to communicate that risks might need to be taken in order to trust Christ. There are no grounds for allowing others to think they can earn salvation by suffering for Jesus.

Luke 14:26, 27, 33
(See also Matt. 10:37-39.)

- "If anyone comes to Me, and does not hate his own father and mother and wife and children and brothers and sisters, yes, and even his own life, he cannot be My disciple. Whoever does not carry his own cross and come after Me cannot be My disciple....So therefore, no one of you can be My disciple who does not give up all his own possessions."

In general the word *disciple* means "a learner and/or follower." The term *disciple* seems to have an elastic definition with various shades of meaning. John 6:66 records that some of Christ's disciples permanently abandoned Him. Apparently, one could be a short-term disciple (learner) without being a believer. However, when the disciples are contrasted with the multitudes that listened to Jesus, these must be believers as in the passages covered in the previous section. (See Mark 8:34; Luke 9:18, 20.) In John 8:31, Christ seems to distinguish between *disciples* and *true disciples*. Those who believe are called to deeper discipleship. The gospels include curious disciples (only learners), convinced disciples (believers), and committed disciples (dedicated believers). Which type of disciples does Jesus have in mind in Luke 14:26ff.? The words in Matt. 10:37-39 are given to believers (i.e., the apostles named in Matt. 10:1-2). Luke 14:25 is addressed to the multitudes. Whether the interpreter takes Luke 14 as a call to become a convinced disciple (believer) or a committed disciple (dedicated believer), the words can not be used to add any condition for salvation beyond faith. We must determine how these teachings could apply to unbelievers and believers (at different stages of spiritual life and development) in ways compatible with salvation by faith.

Misunderstandings

Luke 14:26ff. could be misused to teach that salvation comes by commitment and sacrifice. If the Lord is giving a condition for salvation, then salvation seems to be earned only by the most rigorous of

means. One must suffer and obey to obtain salvation
(v. 27). One must relinquish control of all material
possessions (v. 33). However, what becomes of grace
and of 150 plus texts that condition salvation upon
faith?

Meaning for Unbelievers

If Luke 14:26ff. is viewed as a call to the unsaved,
it is still possible to reconcile the text with the *faith
alone* position. If societal conditions are such that in
order to become a believer one must alienate family,
endure rejection and ridicule, face pain or death
threats (i.e., carry the cross) or lose property, one
must still choose to place faith in Christ. If believing
brings great hardship, one must still believe for salvation comes through faith. Any one among the multitude who had not yet believed had to become a
convinced disciple (believer) whatever the cost or
risk. Beyond this beginning of life in Christ, the Lord
wants even deeper discipleship. There is a difference
between what God requires for salvation (faith) and
what God fully requires to those who have begun to
follow. Unbelievers in the crowd needed to concen-
trate first on overcoming fears in becoming formal
disciples by accepting Jesus as the Messiah.[22] For

---

[22] The author has used the awkward phrase *formal disciple* because the crowds are already disciples in the sense of casual
learners (as in John 6:66). However, most had not made any decision to follow Christ. In another sense these are not really disciples at all. In Luke 14 the Lord calls for total discipleship. For
unbelievers, the deepest part of the message would not be ger-
mane until they made the initial decision to accept Jesus as Savior. At their level Christ primarily wants them to trust Him. The

them this aspect to the discipleship call was most important, but there is more to the Lord's message. For those who had already believed, other aspects to Jesus' call for discipleship were more pertinent.

Meaning for Believers

It is possible that the sermon on discipleship in Luke 14 was given to a mixed crowd. Unbelievers in the audience would need to begin their formal discipleship through faith. The initial entrance was the most important response Jesus wanted from them. The apostles were already convinced disciples. For them (and all others who have received salvation), the Lord's call to committed discipleship impacts them at a different level. The Lord calls them to maintain and increase the level of allegiance they had shown by accepting Him in the first place. Christ requires those already saved to give Him primary allegiance over any other human relationship (v. 26). He asks believers to accept suffering for His sake and wants total obedience (v. 27). He requires that all possessions be placed at His disposal (v. 33). The Lord's call for total discipleship hits the apostles (and other believers) at their more advanced level of spiritual life. For unbelievers, response to that call had to begin with taking risks from a dangerous world in order to believe.

One could prefer to limit the interpretation of Luke 14:26-33 in ways that restrict the Lord's com-

---

apostles had already decided to believe in Him. At their level of spiritual development, Christ's message to them is to continue in fully committed discipleship.

ments to only the unsaved (trust Me whatever the cost) or only the saved (give Me total allegiance). One cannot, however, use Luke 14:26-33 in ways that suggest salvation comes through personal sacrifice, suffering, or obedience.

Lordship Salvation

Saving faith involves acceptance of the fact that Jesus Christ is the Lord (Rom. 10:9; Acts 16:31). Christ must be viewed as God's Son, the Master. This is part of identifying the Biblical Christ. There is also commitment of the soul to Christ for eternal safekeeping. Implied within the act of trusting in Christ for salvation is some desire for deliverance from sin, at the very least a deliverance from sin's penalty. Given that the Old Testament contrasts faith with rebellion, it is unlikely that saving faith can co-exist with an attitude of total rebellion. One who believes Christ is God must also know that he ought to obey Him.

If "Lordship Salvation" involves just these facts, then it could be considered true. However, it is one thing to acknowledge that Christ is the Master and that one ought to obey Him; but it is a vastly different matter to actively obey Him or even promise to obey Him. All Christians would say they should totally obey Christ. None totally obey Christ. Likewise, it is one thing to commit the soul's eternal destiny to Christ but another to yield every area of life to Him. A sinner could even want to obey Christ but not believe he will be able to do so. It must also be remembered that one who can trust in Christ has already desired deliverance from sin to a degree that is sufficient to obtain salvation.

No one will argue that a complete obedience to Christ is a logical and consistent corollary to saving faith. If one commits his soul's eternal destiny to Christ, he should commit everything to Him. If one acknowledges that Christ is God and should be obeyed, the next step should be obedience. However, it is a dangerous mistake to make such a complete obedience or a promise to complete obedience a condition to obtain salvation as those who espouse "Lordship Salvation" often do.

The line, "If Christ is not Lord of all, He is not Lord at all," sounds pious and righteous, but it must be rejected as serious error. First, the New Testament is full of commands to **saved** people urging them to a complete yielding to Christ (e.g., Rom. 6:12-13; 12:1-2; Phil. 3:12-15; James 3:2; 4:8, etc.). Every command implies one could be a believer but not be fully yielded to God; therefore, it is clear that one can be saved without a complete obedience to Christ (though it is not consistent). Secondly, one must insist upon the distinction between what God requires and what He requires for salvation. There are 150 plus verses conditioning salvation upon faith alone. This means that one who trusts in Christ has already acknowledged His Lordship to a sufficient degree and has obeyed to a sufficient degree to obtain salvation. True, God does require a complete submission to the Lordship of Christ, but faith alone is the requirement for salvation. A third problem with Lordship Salvation is that it is a subtle form of works.

Yes, saving faith does involve the attitude that Christ is the Master. Thus, the sinner knows He ought to obey Him. Nevertheless, these aspects of saving faith are simply a realization of the identity of the true Jesus Christ. If one views salvation as contingent upon total obedience to Christ's Lordship or a vow to yield totally to His Lordship, then salvation is based upon human efforts (great human efforts). If one views salvation as based on a less than total yielding to Christ's Lordship, then what is the problem with the view that faith in Christ involves all the yielding to His Lordship that is necessary to provide salvation? The call to yield to the Lordship of Christ is legitimate **if it is not made a condition for salvation**. When complete "Lordship" is tied to salvation, the result is works, i.e., heresy. Finally, Lordship Salvation is ultimately an impossible condition for an unsaved person to fulfill. There is a parallel with the zealous Judaizers who insisted that salvation came from law keeping. Law keeping would be an impossible condition for salvation (Gal. 2:14-16). So is Lordship salvation.

To ask for the forsaking of sin (or the promise to forsake sin) and total submission to Christ's authority (or the vow to submit to Christ's authority) before salvation is to ask the impossible of a sinner. The unsaved person can not break the dominion of sin (John 8:34), and saving faith has no confidence in self to assert that it will vow to overcome sin and obey Christ throughout life. Saving faith entails a realization that Jesus Christ is and ought to be Master. Yet, saving faith is also an attitude of utter helplessness relative to overcoming sin. God requires faith in Christ to be delivered from sin, but not faith in self's ability to make a grandiose promise to forsake and totally yield. Saving faith is not trust in self's power to boast of promises to forsake sin and/or totally obey Christ. It is only after salvation that the power comes to make such a commitment. It is only after salvation that one can have any success in the area of forsaking sin and making Jesus Lord.

The drug addict in a rescue mission may have enough faith to trust in Christ. He believes Jesus Christ is the Lord and desires deliverance from sin. However, when a Christian tells him he must forsake his habit and yield totally in obedience to Christ's Lordship, he is asking the impossible of the poor wretch. The addict knows full well that he cannot forsake his sin, or even honestly promise to forsake it. He may even wish he could make Jesus Lord, but the fact is he cannot, and he knows it. That is why he needs a Savior! Ignorant Christians may tell the man he must forsake sin, promise to quit sinning, make Jesus Lord. Yet, God wants the opposite. He wants the man to feel utterly helpless and hopeless. God wants complete despair of hypocritical and/or boastful promises to change. He wants those trapped in sin to realize that such vows cannot be made in good conscience. God wants the addict and all other sinners to feel that sin is so powerful that only the Lord Jesus Christ could deliver from sin's power, as well as its penalty. God does not require vows of reformation of life for salvation. The opposite attitude of being hopelessly trapped in sin is more compatible with a faith that recognizes utter dependence on the Lord Jesus Christ for all hope of deliverance (first from sin's penalty then its power). Satan might want Christian do-gooders to garble the gospel with additional conditions for salvation. He might want misguided evangelists to require faith in self to make boastful empty vows of reformation. All God requires is that the sinner wants deliverance from sin to the degree of believing in the Lord Jesus Christ and His cross.

Prayer and Saving Faith

Prayer is definitely a God-approved means of expressing faith. In Rom. 10:8 Paul gives his example of how he does evangelism. The phrase, "The word of faith, which we are preaching," could be paraphrased as "The words we use in evangelism to bring about faith." In the following context it is clear that Paul encouraged people to "call upon the name of the Lord" (vv. 12-13) confessing **to God** that Jesus Christ is Lord (v. 9). Probably the best method of evangelism involves instruction that one should pray to express faith in Christ.

However, it is the **faith** expressed by a prayer that saves, not merely prayer. It is not that one can glibly repeat a few lines of some magical prayer to obtain salvation. Apart from the faith expressed by prayer, there is no salvation.

A more fundamental question is "Must there be a prayer in order for there to be salvation?" The key texts that give *faith alone* as the condition for salvation contain virtually no references to prayer. The command is to "believe in Christ" rather than to believe and pray.

Furthermore, a Bible student would be hard pressed to find a point in time when Biblical characters such as Peter, James, and John prayed to obtain salvation. While prayer is the best means to express faith, the condition that brings salvation is **faith** whether a prayer expresses it or not. If a trust in Christ is present, salvation is granted. A prayer expressing this faith is beneficial because it provides assurance to the person that the matter of salvation is settled. However, God knows faith exists in the heart even if it is not directly verbalized by a prayer.

There needs to be balance in the area of prayer and salvation. It is wise to encourage people to pray in order to express faith. However, the fact that a person cannot remember a time of a specific prayer need not be grounds for concluding he or she is unsaved. Many people trust in Christ Jesus for salvation but do not know an exact date or remember a dramatic experience at the beginning of their faith. While it is nice to be able to recall a time when faith began, the matter of overwhelming importance is the presence of faith and not the time it began. If a person can honestly and sincerely maintain he has faith in Christ and His work on the cross, he has salvation. Faith may arise slowly, as it seems to have done with Peter, or faith may arise dramatically as it did with Paul. Salvation is conditioned upon faith. The time of faith's origin and the way it is expressed is secondary to the presence of faith.

Conclusion

All these complex studies end in a simple conclusion with a simple gospel: salvation is conditioned upon faith alone. "Nothing in my hand I bring, simply to Thy cross I cling." Salvation is not offering to God a full hand of a perfect life. Salvation is an empty hand receiving all grace and mercy from the merits of the Savior and His perfect work on the cross.

The type of faith being commanded by the Bible is trust, dependence, and reliance upon Jesus Christ and His work on the cross. Some might ridicule this doctrine as "easy-believism." The Bible calls it grace!